AF586449

Who Killed Napoleon?

10 New Scientific Investigations to Rescue History

Pr Gérard Lucotte, Paris School of Anthropology
& Dr Philippe Bornet

Who Killed Napoleon?

10 New Scientific Investigations to Rescue History

Preface by Pr Jean Tulard

Max Milo

www.maxmilo.com
ISBN: 978-2-31502-170-3

To our mothers.
G.L. and Ph.B.

A child's future is its mother's work.
Napoleon

Acknowledgements

We aknowledge Mr Sou Mong for his precious help and financial support.

The authors would like to thank Pr George Bischopric, Voluntary Assistant Professor, Department of Pathology, University of Miami Miller School of Medicine, *for his translation,*

and

Professor Jean-Noël Fabiani, Emeritus Professor of the History of Medicine, for reviewing chapter 13.

Foreword

Historians rely on documents (charters, treaties, receipts) or testimonies (letters or memoirs). They don't write what they cannot prove always putting documented references at the bottom of the page—those academic footnotes that form the bedrock of scholarship.

In some cases, there is simply no documentary evidence. That's when we have to turn to Science.

To this day, we are still left with important questions about the life of Napoleon Bonaparte. Was he the son of Charles Bonaparte or the Comte de Marbeuf? Was he poisoned with arsenic? If not, what was the illness that took his life? Finally, does he lie in state at Les Invalides, or is this the body of his butler Cipriani?

Numerous investigations of these remaining questions have provided conflicting conclusions. There has been an absence of conclusive documentation.

Professor Gérard Lucotte, head of the Institut d'Anthropologie et de Génétique Moléculaire and a specialist on the Y chromosome, assisted by Dr Philippe Bornet, an historian of Napoleon[1], used hair, skin fragments and samples taken from the Emperor's descendants to tackle these enigmas, which had remained closed to the researcher-historian in the absence of definitive documentation.

Based on their analysis, we finally have definitive conclusions for questions that historians were previously unable to answer.

Clio is silent. Make way for Genetics.

Jean Tulard
of the Académie des Sciences morales et politiques
Professor Emeritus at the Sorbonne

1. Bornet Philippe, *Napoléon et Dieu*, Via Romana, 2021.

1. Introduction

What is the role of genetics, and more generally of science, in historical research? How can these disciplines be applied to the historical questions that still surround Napoleon's life and death to this day given the absence of the documents Professor Tulard refers to? Was the Emperor poisoned with arsenic by General Montholon, in order to inherit the two million francs bequeathed to him in his will, as many French people still believe: "It is not the role of scientists to prove that Napoleon was assassinated. That's the historian's job"[2] claim two well-known historians.

To these historians, I would point out that history is an *assertoric* discipline: it proceeds by alternative propositions. The inevitable complication is that the discussion between the opposing opinions never completely ceases.

2. LENTZ Thierry and MACÉ Jacques, *La mort de Napoléon, mythes, légendes et mystères,* Perrin, 2009, p. 152.

Even if the debate becomes clearer, there will always be a section of readers who refuse to accept the arguments of the other side.

Science, on the other hand, is an *apodictic* discipline[3]. It proceeds humbly and slowly, from the simple to the complex and from the known to the unknown. It measures, quantifies and relies on a series of reproducible and verifiable experiments. The certainties it establishes are definitive and inescapable, barring dishonesty or misinterpretation of the facts.

*

One example: Napoleon's hair is unquestionably rich in arsenic. Work carried out by Dr. Pascal Kintz of the Strasbourg Medical Institute in 2001, at the request of Ben Weider, established that the arsenic in Napoleon's hair was of mineral origin and present in the hair medulla, i.e. it had entered the bloodstream as a result of general intoxication. This would indicate either chronic intoxication or poisoning.

If there was poisoning, the historian is lost in conjecture about the origin of the arsenic: did it come from wallpaper, paint, rat poison?...

3. Apodictic, from the ancient Greek ἀποδεικτικός, is a proposition, a judgment, with the character of universality and absolute necessity, i.e. that which is necessarily true for every mind.

If poisoning has occurred, then the identification of the culprit, the motive for the poisoning and admissible prosecution evidence are missing.

Historians, balancing between these two impossible hypotheses, conclude only with some bad humor that the poisoning thesis is incoherent.

Using the electron microscope, scientific techniques now make it possible to determine the precise location of this arsenic in the hair, which clarifies the origin of the poison. Another enigma: Was Napoleon's body stolen by the British and replaced by that of the butler Cipriani, who had died a little earlier?

Lentz and Macé demonstrate the inconsistencies of this thesis, but are troubled by the disappearance of Cipriani's tomb from the cemetery at Sainte-Hélène. The discovery of Cipriano's body would have definitively eliminated the substitution thesis: "for a scientific or curious mind [...]," they say, "one conclusion is obvious: let's dig up the tomb at Les Invalides"... But, the historians argue, this would be an "unjustified desecration". In short, the historical method has failed. Either the failure is acknowledged, or History trusts Science.

Readers will discover how, with the help of a historian, Science overcame this obstacle, with a required degree of audacity. We shall also see that science can ratify the judgment of history. For example, the death mask cast by

François Antommarchi, the Emperor's doctor at St. Helena, is indeed a "reconstruction [which] does not represent Napoleon's face", but was made from an authentic cast. It thus provides a new degree of certainty.

What, other than Science could have discovered the origin of Napoleon's distant ancestors by determining the so-called *haplotype*[4]? Who could have questioned the salacious rumors, insulting to the Emperor's memory, and widely repeated by Anglo-Saxon news sources, claiming that his penis had ended up in the curiosity cabinet of an American urologist? Who could have denied or confirmed the parentage of Louis Bonaparte, King of Holland, of Prince Napoleon, descendant of Jerome, of the current Count Walewski and of the still unknown American Mike Davis? How can we explain the body's astonishing preservation in a tropical climate, and, *last but not least,* elucidate **the true cause of Napoleon's death**? Without the scientific techniques of today, it would not be possible.

For twelve years, from 2010 to 2022, no less than a dozen scientific investigations were carried out, with the help of Prince Charles Napoléon (descendant of the Emperor through the branch descended from Jérôme Bonaparte, the Emperor's youngest brother) and Count Walewski

4. A haplotype is a set of genes located on the same chromosome and transmitted to descendants.

(descendant of a natural son of Napoléon I). Thanks to his genetics laboratory and electron microscope, we have accomplished a gigantic feat that will astound all Napoleon enthusiasts.

*

Before I present the results of our work, let me tell you a little about my family origins and professional background. The Lucottes are Burgundians, originally from the canton of Arnay-le-Duc, in what is now the Côte-d'Or department. Burgundy was a province that always appealed to Napoleon Bonaparte, who wanted to acquire property there when he was still a general. A letter from him to his secretary Bourienne was found on this subject. A Claude Lucotte, a laborer, had settled there at the end of the reign of Louis XIV, giving rise to a whole line of Lucottes, the most famous of whom, an Empire general and friend of General Hugo (Victor's father), gave his name to an old street in the 15th arrondissement of Paris[5].

5. Rue du Général-Lucotte, in the 15th arrondissement of Paris, began on rue Lucien-Bossoutrot and ended on avenue de la Porte-de-Sèvres. After serving as a service road for the maintenance workshops of tramway line 3, it disappeared in the new headquarters of the French Ministry of Defense.

The Burgundians, a race reputed for their wit, and once subjects of Charles the Bold, are heirs to the hourglass-shaped kingdom of Lotharingia, founded by Lothaire II (855-869), It stretched from the Black Forrest (in French, *Les Vosges*) to Friesland and encompassing present-day Lorraine(the name derived from the name of the kingdom) to the Duchy of Burgundy which also gave birth to Flanders, a place of people both hedonists and mystics.

My father was a surgeon and I began studying medicine myself, although I soon realized that I preferred biology to the chill of the medical clinic.

After obtaining a doctorate in genetics and then a doctorate in science—a diploma which, at the time, required fifteen years' work on my thesis—I began my professional career at the CNRS in Gif-sur-Yvette, before becoming head of department at the Centre National de Transfusion Sanguine, on rue Alexandre-Cabanel in Paris. It was a difficult time back in those years of the HIV-contaminated blood scandal, when hemophiliacs were waiting for us at the hospital exits to tear up their blood group cards and spit on us.

In 1982, I founded one of France's very first human molecular genetics laboratories in Paris, where I discovered the DNA markers of the Y chromosome, nicknamed (for one of its forms) "Abraham's chromosome." I became a professor at the Paris School of Anthropology, a post I've held for the rest of my life, and founded the Institute of Anthropology and Molecular Genetics.

Physically, of average height, I've grown a mustache and now wear my hair long, as a mark of academic authority. Morally, I loathe naggers, chatterboxes and curmudgeons of all stripes who claim to dictate what I should think.

The subject of Napoleon hadn't yet crossed my path when everything changed, thanks to a psychic...

*

The text we are about to read is intended to be accessible to anyone who has had a scientific education in secondary school. The passages in the notes and appendices are intended more specifically for scientists, who should read them before referring to my articles.

2. How it all Began

As always, it all began with a woman.

Three dynasties now claim to have the right to rule France in the unlikely event of the Republic's demise.

Prince Jean d'Orléans or Jean de France, the Orleanist pretender, born 1965, son of Henri d'Orléans, Count of Paris (died January 21, 2019, the anniversary the death of of Louis XVI), descended from Louis XIV's younger brother Philippe, Duke of Orléans.

Louis de Bourbon, born in 1974, son of the Duc d'Anjou, is a direct descendant of Louis XIV. His ancestor Philippe de France had to renounce his rights to the French crown at the time of the Treaty of Utrecht in 1713 in order to ascend the Spanish throne.

Jean-Christophe Napoléon, born in 1986, is a descendant of Jérôme Bonaparte, and upon his father's death will bear the title of Prince Napoléon, as has been the rule since

Napoléon III. It is notable that his mother is a Bourbon of the Kingdom of the Two Sicilies, and that he married Olympia von Arco-Zinneberg, a Habsburg (Marie-Louise must have been pleased!), herself a descendant of two French kings, Charles X and Louis-Philippe. He was preferred by his grandfather over his father Charles as heir to the imperial throne, because of the latter's divorce and his political positions close to the socialist left. Both are descendants of Jérôme Bonaparte, Napoleon I's youngest brother.

Charles Bonaparte had a twin sister, Princess Catherine, who worked as a social worker, and was a friend of Patricia Darré, the journalist, writer and medium. Darré has written several books about her paranormal experiences, published by Michel Lafon, and she has appeared as a guest of Stéphane Bern and Nikos Aliagas on their radio and television broadcasts. She claims to have been in contact with historical figures such as... Napoleon, who informed her that his remains did not lie in Les Invalides, and that he did not appreciate his memory being venerated in a place when his remains were elsewhere.

*

In the 2010s, the theory that the British had substituted Napoleon's body was still widely believed. Princess Catherine, endowed with a fine, feminine, nervous nature (and, perhaps guilt-ridden by the thought that she had done nothing for the memory of her glorious ancestor) gathered the *crème de la crème* of Napoleonâtres and Bonapartophiles at the Hôtel Lutetia to debate the subject of the location of Napoleons remains.

Among that group of specialists, the curious, and journalists, were historians such as the renowned David Chanteranne of the *Souvenir napoléonien* and Jean-François Prévost, professor of constitutional law and European law at Dauphine—a friend of the writer Didier Van Cauwelaert—and member of the Institut d'Anthropologie et de Génétique Moléculaire, of which I am the founder.

Pr Prévost had invited me to this meeting as a geneticist with a passion for what is known as "genetics at the service of history," or historical genetics, sometimes referred to as "recreational" genetics (the word "recreational" is a poor translation of English, meaning that this type of genetics is interested in unusual subjects outside its ordinary field of action). This "recreational" genetics is certainly a lot of fun, but in fact it's not recreational at all, and requires—and I can testify to this!—It has helped to unravel some historical mysteries, such as the identification of the bodies of the Romanovs, liquidated by the Soviets.

Collector Pierre-Jean Chalençon, the famous blond-haired TV host (who has since been accused of organizing clandestine dinners during confinement) was willing to provide hair from Napoleon's sister Caroline. I asked as well for a certified copy of Napoleon's own hair.

As I learned at the meeting, the Châteauroux museum possessed a reliquary that belonged to Vivant Denon, the first director of the Musée du Louvre, and contained a lock of Napoleon's hair. The engraver Vivant Denon (1747-1825) headed Louis XVI's Cabinet des Médailles. He was surprised by the Revolution while in Italy and, was considered a refugee there ; he only was able to return to France with the protection of the painter David, a friend of General Bonaparte, whom he is said to have met in a milliner's store as early as 1793. He took part in the Egyptian campaign and became director of the museum that was to become our Louvre until 1815.

Could a genetic identification be attempted from this sample? Napoleon and Caroline must both have carried the mitochondrial DNA (mtDNA for short) bequeathed by their mother Letizia. This mtDNA is transmitted to all children, male and female, in the first generation. Its study could provide an initial marker, enabling formal identification. Three other teams previously consulted on this subject had failed before me. Funding of €5,000 from Princess Catherine was available. I took up the challenge.

*

The Musée de Châteauroux is a municipal museum, and as such depends, on the town for support. Not part of the National Museums, Its holdings come primarily from General Bertrand, to whom we owe the famous bridge over the Danube before the Battle of Wagram in 1809, and who, along with his family, was one of the Emperor's unfortunate companions.

Bertrand left his *Cahiers* in stenographic form, which were very difficult to read and were published late, from 1949 onwards. A fully restored version has been published by François Houdecek, of the Fondation Napoléon, on the bicentenary of Napoleon's death in 2021. Bertrand had witnessed Napoleon's last moments, signed the minutes of his burial and formally acknowledged his death in 1840 Napoleon's remains were returned to France.

At the time, Michèle Naturel was director of the Musée Bertrand, which occupies General Henri-Gatien Bertrand's mansion (built by his grandfather in the 18th century), and which received numerous bequests from other collectors, including bibliophile Jean-Louis Bourdillon (1782-1856), collector Vivie de Régie and a descendant of the Thabaud Boislareine-Desaix family. Among the objects bequeathed were souvenirs that had belonged to Vivant Denon, a box containing hair from the mummified body of Letizia (Napoleon's mother) and two death masks of the Emperor.

I got back in touch with Mme Naturel, whose acquaintance I had made at the Méridien-Montparnasse meeting and, despite unseemly pressure from unscrupulous competitors, which she heroically resisted, with the support of her municipality, I was able (perhaps guided by the spirits of Napoleon!) to come to Châteauroux, Patricia Darré's native capital in the Berry region, where enchanters and sorcerers once swarmed, to examine Vivant Denon's reliquary, and then to have the box containing the hair of Napoleon's mother opened in front of me...

*

Since the Covid-19 epidemic, everyone has heard of PCR as a means of identifying this coronavirus from its RNA. In good French, we should say ACP, "Amplification en chaine polymerase" Amplification, because the DNA fragment (the same applies to RNA in the case of covid-19) is duplicated at each cycle: the two DNA strands give 4, 8, 16, 32, etc. under the effect of DNA Polymerase enzyme, which triggers the biochemical reaction leading to enough DNA molecules for biochemical analysis.

DNA (deoxyribonucleic acid) is a double-spiral molecule. Imagine a ladder with rungs, each twisted on itself. Each side is spiral-shaped and rotates around the other. The four building blocks of DNA are: adenine, thymine, cytosine and guanine, designated by their initials: A, T, C and G. Adenine pairs with thymine and cytosine with guanine. A-T and C-G form so many "rungs" on the DNA ladder, allowing the two DNA "struts" to come together.

A, T, C and G form the letters of an alphabet that can be used to write sentences, paragraphs, pages and tomes of a genetic encyclopedia containing the information necessary for life. Some passages are identical for all human beings, others vary. We're all human, but we're also all different (except for identical twins).

Chromosomes are made up of DNA and reside in the cell nucleus. An important exception is the mitochondria, the energy factories of the cell, which are located located outside the nucleus in the cytoplasm, and which contain their own unique fragments of DNA known as "mitochondrial DNA (mtDNA)." While half the chromosomes in the nucleus are composed of paternal and maternal DNA, mtDNA comes *exclusively from the mother*. It's the female counterpart of the Y chromosome, which comes *only from the father*, as only men have one.

Another particularity of this mtDNA is that it is fairly abundant in cells, making it easier to analyze.

*

The Vivant Denon reliquary in the Musée de Châteauroux contains a lock of Napoleon's hair, and its authentication is beyond doubt ; it is accompanied by a letter signed by Napoleon. I also found Letizia's hair in Châteauroux.

*

When two human beings reproduce, each donates a copy of his or her chromosomes, but when this happens, errors sometimes occur that may become hereditary. These are known as mutations. A mutation is defined by a change from one base to another, at a precise point on the DNA molecule, for example at the 2582nd position in the reading direction. The mtDNA can also mutate, as can the Y chromosome.

But how does PCR work in practice? The technique was developed by Kary Mullis in the 1980s, for which he was awarded the Nobel Prize in 1993.

The first step is to separate the two strands of DNA by heating it to 93-96°C. Next, two "primers" are deposited on one of the strands, indicating the beginning and end of the DNA passage to be copied; for this, the temperature is lowered to 55-65°C. Finally, nucleotides and DNA polymerase are added when the temperature is raised to 72°C. These three phases constitute a cycle, at the end of which the number of chains has doubled. After 20 cycles, one million copies are theoretically available, as the number of copies increases exponentially. However, as the yield of a cycle is not 100%, in practice 35 to 40 cycles are required.

This process is now automated to achieve the required temperature variations as quickly as possible. Another advance is the use of a polymerase discovered in a bacterium capable of thriving at temperatures in excess of 90°C, eliminating the need to add polymerase to the mixture at each cycle.

In the past, it was only possible to conclude whether a DNA sequence was present or absent. Today, it is possible to quantify its presence.

The number 1 concern of laboratories processing old DNA is the possibility of contamination by other biological material. If a technician sneezes on the sample or scratches his or her scalp, dropping a few skin cells, then contamination and error have occurred.

Naturally, all the necessary precautions were taken, details of which can be found in my 2010 article[6]: gloves and masks, irradiated pipette tips, sterile hoods... The samples

6. LUCOTTE Gérard, "A rare variant of the mtDNA HVS1 sequence in the hairs of Napoleon's family", *Investigative Genetics*, vol.1, 2010, p. 1-5.

were studied in separate laboratories accustomed to this especially delicate work with ancient DNA.

*

The mtDNA fragment studied was located between positions 15,991 and 16,390, a particularly variable part of the genomic sequence. In 1981, Anderson and his colleagues at Cambridge described the 16,569 bases that make up human mtDNA, three tightly written pages in a scientific journal. If there is a change from Anderson's sequence, it is called a mutation.

At position 16184, the *cytosine* in Letizia's, Napoleon's and Caroline's mtDNA has been replaced by a *thymine:*

16184 C->T

Or, in simpler terms:

16184 T

Figure 1 (see appendix) shows this mutation, as described in the original article. But is this mutation frequent or rare? First of all, I consulted the *Federal Bureau of Investigation* database, which contains almost five thousand mtDNA sequences useful in police investigations: it didn't appear (a frequency - i.e. the inverse of the percentage - of less than 0.02%)! In another database, *EMPOP*, only three individuals out of 4775 had this 16184C->T mutation, i.e. a frequency of 0.067%. My colleague Dr. Pala (in a personal communication) assured me that she had found it in only three samples: one in Crete and two in Italy, out of the 37,000 in her database, i.e. a frequency of around 0.008%[7].

A mutation is characterized by its frequency. The rarer it is, the less likely it is to be found in two samples by chance (i.e. the same individual or two closely related relatives). The discovery of this same mutation (present in Letizia, Napoleon and Caroline) will in future make it possible to identify any biological material (skin, hair, bone, tendon) as belonging or not to Napoleon, with such a high probability that it will be tantamount to virtual certainty. I had the fulcrum, as Archimedes used to say!

But to validate this transfer, didn't we need authorization to access the tomb *at Les Invalides?*

---

7. *Op. cit.*

3. Is Napoleon's Body in Westminster Abbey?

On April 26, 1821, on St. Helena, the remote South Atlantic island where Napoleon was exiled after Waterloo, General Montholon, who had become his nurse, entered the dying Napoleon's room at four o'clock in the morning:

"The Emperor said to me with remarkable emotion: *I've just seen my good Josephine, but she didn't want to kiss me ; she pulled away just as I wanted to take her in my arms. She was sitting there, as if I'd seen her the day before. She hasn't changed: still the same, still devoted to me. She told me we'd see each other again and never leave each other. She assures me that... Have you seen her?* I was very careful not to say anything to her that might increase the feverish exaltation that was all too obvious to me. I made him drink his potion, changed him, and he fell asleep; but when he woke up, he told me again about Joséphine, and I would have agitated him for no reason had I told him it was only a dream".

These end-of-life experiences are frequent and soothing; they are not hallucinations, which are also frequent, but are less elaborate and not perceived as disturbing or frightening[8]. **It was only at this point that** Napoleon began to become delirious at times.

On April 27, Napoleon dictated a letter for Montholon to send to Lowe, announcing his death.

On April 28, the Emperor ordered his physician Antommarchi to carry out an autopsy after his death, to examine his stomach thoroughly and make a precise report to his son, in case he had hereditary stomach cancer. Despite his reluctance, he took the living room as his bedroom. During the night, he talked sadly with Montholon about the death of all the men he had known, especially Lannes, Crétin[9]... He spoke like a man who has lost his memory and gone deaf.

On April 29, Montholon tried to get him to sign one last paper, but Napoleon could no longer see the Grand Marshal Bertrand in front of him. Bertrand, who had had harsh words for Napoleon a few days earlier, cried: "Voilà le grand Napoléon, misérable, humble".

---

8. FENWICK Peter (Dr), *When the end of life approaches*, horizonresearch.org, The Art of Dying, Continuum Books, 2008.
9. Officer killed at the battle of Aboukir.

On April 30, the Emperor was lucid and woke up shouting: "Ah! ah! la mort!" He told Montholon: "Mon ami, je suis mort" ("My friend, I'm dead"). Antommarchi thought he was going to pass, between ten and eleven o'clock.

But on May 1, Napoleon was still alive. At two o'clock in the afternoon, the fever subsided. Abbé Vignali, his chaplain, had the altar set up and spent a few moments alone with the Emperor to give him extreme unction. Everyone withdrew, leaving Vignali alone to join the others a few moments later in the next room.

In his *Mémoires,* Marchand places this episode on May 3, which is a mistake. Bertrand places it on May 1, and Marchand himself, in a letter to Chevalier de Beauterne, mentions May 1. The May 1st date is also more logical, as Napoleon had almost died the day before. According to Marchand's valet de chambre, half an hour later, the Abbé came out and told him: "The Emperor has just been administered, the state of his stomach does not allow any other sacrament". On the subject of communion, Ali and Marchand concur in their account of the intervention of Abbé Vignali, who was summoned to the Emperor's bedside, but Marchand specifies that the Abbé "in bourgeois attire", was holding something underneath which he was trying to conceal, and which I did not try to guess, thinking that he had just performed a religious act". Vignali began the Quarante-Heures prayers.

On May 2, Napoleon repeated his request to examine his stomach and compare the findings with his father's autopsy report. The doctor and the two generals were at their wits' end. In the middle of the night, Napoleon wanted to get up. Montholon and Vignali took him by the arm. Vignali left him, knelt down and prayed. The Emperor sighed loudly, with effort, and then said: "Mon Dieu ! My God! My God!" Antommarchi took his pulse and found that it was up to 108 per minute. The patient had probably gone into atrial fibrillation.

On May 3, there was a short-lived improvement.

*

On May 5, Vignali was present, along with the others. The Bertrand children burst into the room. They didn't recognize the emperor! At 5:49 in the afternoon, Napoleon died. Grand Marshal Bertrand closed his eyes. At 10 a.m., Abbé Vignali said a few prayers.

May 6: the autopsy took place at 2 pm., in front of seventeen witnesses. Meanwhile, Abbé Vignali was on his knees at the foot of the altar. The weather was heavy and hot. At 4 p.m., Napoleon already looked older than his fifty-two years. He had been dressed in the uniform of colonel of the Imperial Guard chasseurs, probably with his "Grand cordon" of the Legion of Honor on his sash.

By May 7, the decaying body stank. A death mask was taken, but the features were soft and unattractive, as the necessary plaster had not been found immediately.

The coffin was closed at 7pm. A report was drawn up, signed by Bertrand, Montholon and Marchand. Here is this key document, reproduced by historian[10] Bruno Roy-Henry:

> *This day of today, the seventh of May, one thousand eight hundred and twenty-one, at Longwood, island of Saint Helena, the body of Emperor Napoleon, dressed in the uniform of the chasseurs de la garde, was laid in a tin coffin [...].*
>
> *This first coffin, having been soldered in our presence, was placed inside a lead coffin, which, having also been soldered, was enclosed in a third mahogany coffin.*

The existence of these three coffins is attested by the Marquis de Montchenu, Louis XVIII's commissioner, and the island's governor, Hudson Lowe. Three coffins: pewter, lead and mahogany.

In the first coffin were his hat, placed at his feet, and two vases containing his heart and stomach respectively.

---

10. ROY-HENRY Bruno, *Napoléon, l'énigme de l'exhumé de Sainte-Hélène*, L'Archipel, 2003.

On May 9, the coffin was placed with great pomp in the Vallée des Géraniums, near a spring whose water Napoleon had enjoyed on horseback. Every measure was taken to protect the coffin from humidity. The huge stone closing the coffin was cemented in place.

On March 27, Napoleon had confided to Bertrand: "The only thing to fear is that the English might want to keep my corpse and put it in Westminster." On April 13, he repeated: "I have just written to the Prince Regent to ask him not to keep my ashes in London".

*

King Louis-Philippe, who had judged Napoleon severely in his youth, agreed, following intrigues from his entourage too long to recount, to have Napoleon's remains repatriated to France from St Helena. He announced his decision on his own birthday, May 1, 1840. As the mission was diplomatically more delicate than it appeared, he was joined by Louis-Philippe's son, the Prince de Joinville, a naval officer in command of *La Belle-Poule,* Count Philippe de Rohan-Chabot, whose grandmother was Lady Fitzgerald, which earned him many alliances and connections across the Channel.

The mission was a delicate one for two reasons.

1. The French wanted to confirm the identity of the body being handed over to them, and any discrepancies could have been embarrassing for to the English, so the expedition set off to France with the surviving witnesses to Napoleon's captivity, including Bertrand, Gourgaud, Las Cases fils, and Marchand. It was likely that the decomposition of the body had left only a skeleton, and that it would be necessary to verify items in the coffin that would be remembered only by close friends.

2. Diplomatic relations between France and England were strained, as Mehmet Ali, an ally of France, wanted to proclaim Egypt's independence from the Ottoman Empire, which London objected to, with the support of Russia. Public opinion in France was bellicose. What would happen if the rumor that Napoleon's body had been stolen by the British was confirmed by the discovery of a body other than that of the Emperor? Could a war break out, a war for which France was unprepared?

A number of curious events occurred.

1. *La Belle-Poule* sailed from Toulon on July 7, 1840, and didn't make landfall until October 8. *The Oreste* was dispatched to catch up with *La Belle-Poule*, on the pretext of bringing her a pilot, more probably, to deliver a secret letter to the Prince of Joinville.

2. Sir Middlemore, Governor of St. Helena, had made no provision for exhumation or for the body's recovery. He

refused any help from the French troops. Did England have something to hide?

3. Prince de Joinville strictly confined his troops to the ship, a severe hardship for men who hadn't been ashore for over three months ! He himself remained aboard the frigate. What was there to fear, when Chabot had toasted the "indissoluble union of France and England"? Ensign Pujol, who wanted to report the event, was furious: all drawings and photographs were forbidden. However, a daguerreotype and a large number of plates had been planned. They were of no use. Draughtsman Henri Durand-Brager, who was to draw the most important scenes, was confined to the ship like the others. Rohan-Chabot wrote to Thiers on October 28: "in accordance with your orders, no other person (other than those authorized) has been introduced in the name of France into the enclosure reserved around the tomb". Were the French afraid of discovering something?

*

At midnight on October 15, 1840, eighteen Frenchmen gathered for the ceremony. Present were the workman who had soldered the tin and lead coffins in 1821, and Andrew Darling, who had made the mahogany coffin. After nine hours' work in the rain, the vault was opened. Naval surgeon Guillard jumped into the sepulchre and purified it with chlorine. A priest was present: Abbé Coquereau, who consecrated the place with holy water. Joinville was notified by a bill. Rohan-Chabot wrote to him:

> *I can't unlock the lock on the ebony coffin [...]. Soldiers saw through the side of the mahogany case [...]. They remove the lead coffin and place it in the ebony sarcophagus [...]. Three cases remain to be opened: one of lead, one of wood, one of tin [...]. The coffin solder is slowly cut away, and the lid carefully lifted [...]. The doctor lifts [the padded satin] to reveal Napoleon's body...*

Where did this fourth wooden coffin come from, sandwiched between lead and tin?

*

What's more, the body is intact. How can a body remain intact for twenty years in a tropical climate? If not a miracle, at least an enigma.

*

Journalist and collector Georges Rétif de la Bretonne[11] presented a comprehensive thesis on the replacement of Napoleon's body by the English.

Rétif first explains that the French replaced Napoleon's death mask with that of Cipriani, his butler, who died in 1818, because the Emperor's features were too altered and risked giving posterity a bad image of him. The English learned of this and noticed that not only the mask, but also Cipriani's body could pass for that of Napoleon. They substituted the body of one for that of the other and sent Napoleon's to England, where the ghastly, purportedly necrophagous, King George IV would have delighted in it.

In 1840, the witnesses, duly warned by Joinville of the risk of diplomatic complications, and paralyzed by the prospect of seeing their historical mask deception uncovered, feigned recognition of Napoleon and remained silent, even though they had not recognized the Emperor's body in the few minutes it took to identify it.

Cipriani was probably one of Napoleon's spies, who had become a double agent and gone over to the service of the British. When he was revealed as a double agent, he committed suicide by arsenic in 1818. His body was dressed in Napoleon's clothes, while Napoleon's body was sent to Westminster.

---

11. RÉTIF DE LA BRETONNE Georges, *Anglais, rendez-nous Napoléon... Napoléon n'est pas aux Invalides,* Jérôme Martineau, éditeur, 1969.

An intriguing fact: director Terence Young, author of the first *James Bond* films and great-grandson of Sergeant John Young, who stood guard at Napoleon's tomb on St. Helena, once confided to Rétif that his grandmother, while showing him around Westminster, had told him that Napoleon's body lay beneath her feet.

It was easy to convince Rétif of the falsity of the substitution theory: all he had to do was find Cipriani's body. But when Gilbert Martineau, the French consul, searched for him in the Jamestown cemetery... his grave had disappeared!

*

To put an end to speculation once and for all, one conclusion seemed obvious: open the tomb at Les Invalides and carry out genetic analysis. Historians Lentz and Macé choked with indignation at this prospect, concluding in 2009: "The thesis of substitution rests entirely on a biased or incomplete reading of the sources and on the imagination of its creators [...], Napoleon's tomb is not that of Mr. Everyman," and even speaking of opening the tomb is unjustified desecration[12].

12. LENTZ Thierry, MACÉ Jacques, *La mort de Napoléon, mythes, légendes et mystères*, Perrin, 2009, p. 215.

*

My friend, the historian Roy-Henry, had discovered that a fragment of the Emperor's skin was once on display in the showcase dedicated to the *Retour des Cendres*, in the Salle Bugeaud, reference 05673, captioned "Morceau d'épiderme détaché du visage de l'Empereur" ("Piece of epidermis detached from the Emperor's face").

With Jacques Macé, whose acquaintance I had made at that infamous meeting at the Hôtel Méridien-Montparnasse, I learned that this skin fragment had been removed by Dr. Guillard. Indeed, when Guillard had opened the coffin and rolled up the gauze covering the body, he had surreptitiously removed a fragment of the Emperor's skin, brought it back to Paris and inserted it in a medallion. However, this fragment was no longer on display at the Invalides, but in the reserves of the Musée de l'Armée at Satory. Napoleon III had given it to his equerry, Firmin Rainbeaux, and one of Rainbeaux's descendants donated it to the Musée de l'Armée in 1936.

*

Satory is a district of Versailles where various army organizations are located, including a military camp. It also bears the memory of Clément Ader, who, in 1897, was the first to launch a "heavier-than-air" aircraft. Many Communards were executed there by firing squad, including Louis Rossel, and Louise Michel was imprisoned there. Some scenes from the film *L'armée des ombres* were shot on the site where the firing squad did its work, leaving Satory with a slightly sinister history.

General Bresse and Mr. Guillet, military and civilian directors respectively of the Musée des Armées, having authorized us to *examine* this skin fragment, I went there for the first time, accompanied by Jacques Macé. The fragment was housed in an 18-carat gold and glass medallion, with a button clasp that I made sure was still functional. Figure 2 (see appendix) shows the front and back of the medallion.

In this medallion, I was to find traces of silica and calcium, alumina and aluminum silicate, as well as animal glue. All this dust can easily be collected with *scotch-tape*. You should know, dear reader, that alumina and aluminum silicate are typical of lava from the volcanic island of St. Helena.

Macé took numerous photos ; the handwriting on the label was similar to that left in the archives of the Château de Vincennes by Dr. Guillard, with the same *d's* and *r's*.

It all sounded very promising.

*

I resolved to return to the museum alone, with the firm intention of unravelling the mystery. Like the first time, I was ushered into a room and left alone. Like the first time, our interlocutors seemed to have been recruited from the staff rather than from the first line of management.

I had with me a pair of sterile gloves, forceps and blade. I opened the medallion. The fragment was resting on a piece of onyx. Without trembling, I cut two tiny fragments at the edge of the anatomical piece and took two dust samples. No sooner had I closed the medallion than a tall, slender black woman in uniform burst into the room with an air of suspicion. Clearly, she had received last-minute cautionary instructions from her superiors, and asked me if I had taken any samples. She replied that I had, and urged me to return them to her. Without resisting, I gave her one of the two *scotch-tapes*, the other precious samples remaining in the bottom of my satchel.

The rest of the interview was rather cold. I left without question. As I made my way out, an alarm siren tore through the air. For a moment, I thought I was in for a body search and incarceration in a military security cell. Would Professor Lucotte be shot on the front line in front of the statue of Napoleon in the courtyard of Les Invalides? Fortunately, this was not to be...

To those who would criticize me for having done as I did, I would reply that I had authorization to *examine* the skin fragment. According to the CNRTL definition (Centre National de Ressources Textuelles et Lexicales, created in 2005 by the CNRS), *to examine* is "to examine something attentively, at length, carefully, attentively, methodically, in detail, closely, from every angle, in every aspect, with a magnifying glass, under a microscope". The doctor studies with his eyes, but also with his microscope, and takes samples from the patient's body. So, as my predecessors Drs. Antommarchi and Guillard had done, I took a sample and studied it carefully and meticulously.

*

I was already in possession of the formula for Napoleon's mitochondrial DNA. It was a simple matter to identify the skin fragment: it was indeed the emperor Napoleon Bonaparte[13]. Napoleon sleeps his last under the dome of the Invalides, next to his son, the Duc de Reichstadt, his friend Bertrand and the Maréchal de Turenne, whom he had brought in himself.

Thierry Lentz may have added a new episode to his "chronicle of the grumpy", but I had acted for the discovery

13. LUCOTTE Gérard, THOMASSET Thierry, BORENSZTAJN Stephen, "The medallion of Dr Rémy Guillard (1799-1869) Contains Well Epidermis of Napoleon the First", *International Journal of Sciences*, vol.10 (11), november 2021.

of historical truth, and genetics had won one of its greatest victories. I received no comments from the museum or the army. If I had proved that Napoleon's body was at Westminster, I would have disgraced Les Invalides and caused an international scandal, I would have been condemned to the gallows, but since Napoleon was indeed on the banks of the Seine, "in the midst of the people he had loved so much", the army breathed a sigh of relief. I think I even deserved a medal. What is the Minister of Defense waiting for?

*

But how to explain the four-coffin blunder? Andrew Darling, in his diary, reports having ordered four coffins with the help of Captain Benett, who sacrificed the mahogany table in his dining room: "The set should consist of 1° a satin-lined tin coffin, 2° a wooden coffin, 3° a lead coffin, then 4° another mahogany one, which was carried out.

Darroch confirms: "The first is tinplate, the second mahogany, the third lead and the fourth mahogany.

Marchand, in his *Mémoires,* also mentions four coffins.

Antommarchi, in 1825, confirms the four coffins: tinplate, mahogany, lead and mahogany.

The tin coffin was tightly fitted into the wooden one, and the two of them seemed to be one. Those who haven't seen anything up close and talk without knowing only remember the three materials used: tin, lead and mahogany. That's why some have spoken of three coffins.

4. Was Napoleon Poisoned?

If Napoleon really did die of cancer, as the English claim, why was he still so fat at the end of his life? Dr. Alessandro Lugli, from the Institute of Pathology at the University of Basel, measured the waistlines of 12 pairs of pants worn by Napoleon Bonaparte between 1800 and 1821: he put on between 67 and 90 kg between 1800 and 1820 for 1.67 m, and lost 11 kg again in the year of his death, still weighing 79 kg, i.e. some 15 kg overweight. Napoleon did not die cachectic, as cancer patients usually are at the end of their lives. So, how did it go?

Napoleon and poison is a recurring theme in our hero's life ! Speaking of poisoning, if we are to believe the historian G. Lenôtre, the young Napoleon had already been the victim of a poisoning attempt by a jealous woman.

He also attempted suicide by poison in 1814. In fact, during the night of April 11 to 12, 1814, he took from his kit a sachet, present since the retreat from Russia, containing a substance that was supposed to render death instantaneous: he used it, but either it had lost its strength, or his stomach had convulsed too soon, and he vomited the poison, avoiding he fate he had expected. At 11 o'clock in the evening, he sent for the Duke of Bassano, the Duke of Vicenza, the Count of Turenne and Count Bertrand, told them of the attempt he had made, and said: "God does not want this"[14].

He would later repeat: "God did not want me to die again. Saint Helena was in my destiny"[15].

But on June 28 or 29, 1815, he was still thinking about it, and his valet Marchand testified: "He gave me a small bottle, fifteen lines long and four or five wide, containing a red liqueur, advising me not to let anyone see it, and added: *Make sure I have it with me.* And as he realized how deeply my soul was afflicted, he pressed his hand to my cheek"[16]...

*

14. MARCHAND Louis Joseph, *Mémoires*, tome I, Tallandier, 1991, p. 20.
15. MONTHOLON, *Napoléon à Sainte-Hélène*, tome 9, p. 594.
16. MARCHAND Louis Joseph, *op. cit.* p. 187.

In Sweden, a historical investigation completed in 1958, proved that King Erik XIV had been poisoned with arsenic by his brother John in 1577. Forshufvud, a Swedish stomatologist from Gothenburg, obtained a hair from the shaved imperial skull the day after the king's death, and had it tested for arsenic: the level was ten times higher than what is considered normal today.

In 1961, the account of a judicial inquiry into Napoleon's death was published by Plon, written by the same Dr. Sten Forshufvud[17]. Forshufvud, who spoke French after studying in Bordeaux and who had had a passion for the history of the First Empire, had read Marchand's *Mémoires* as soon as they appeared in 1955. These *memoirs* provided precise medical details of Napoleon's death, which he interpreted as signs of arsenic poisoning.

Ben Weider was a Canadian businessman who made his fortune selling bodybuilding supplements, was Arnold Schwarzenegger's sponsor, and a virtuoso communicator. President of the Souvenir napoléonien de Montréal and then of an international Napoleonic Society, he met Forshufvud in the 1970s. In France, another "conspiracy theorist", René Maury, also took up the poisoning thesis

17. FORSHUFVUD Sten, *Was Napoleon poisoned? Une enquête judiciaire*, Paris, Plon, 1961.

in 1994[18], then in two other books, the last of which was written by a descendant of General de Montholon.

But who would have directed the poisoning? The English? The Comte d'Artois (brother of Louis XVIII and future King Charles X)? Or Montholon on his own initiative?

To supporters of the idea of a conspiracy to poison Napoleon, Montholon was the primary "person of interest." He had the key to the cellar, saw the Emperor every day, had proved an understanding caretaker, and was listed as the beneficiary of two million francs in Napoleon's will. Arsenic is widely used as rat poison on the rodent-infested island, so he would have had access.

Ben Weider ordered a new arsenic assay from the FBI laboratory, and in June 2001, he launched a major press campaign in support of his latest book on the subject. In addition, he asked Dr. Pascal Kintz, Professor of Forensic Medicine at the Strasbourg Institute of Forensic Medicine and President of the French Society of Toxicology to verify his assays using another method: nuclear physics.

How can physics help chemistry? A neutron bombardment excites the electrons orbiting an atom. The energized electrons change orbit as they move away from the nucleus. They then return to their initial orbit, emitting radiation of a wavelength characteristic of the bombarded element.

18. Maury René, *L'assassin de Napoléon ou le mystère de Sainte-Hélène*, Paris, Albin Michel, 1994.

After this study, Kintz asserted that the arsenic present in Napoleon's hair:

1. It was of mineral origin (in other words, it did not come from organic products);
2. That it had attached itself to the *medulla* (center) of the hair bulb, proving that it had been integrated from arsenic circulating in the blood.

It was a strong argument for intoxication, if not deliberate poisoning ! Readers are well aware of the difference between intoxication, which is involuntary, and poisoning, which is voluntary and presupposes a criminal plan[19].

*

It should also be noted that the current consensus is that the *normal concentration* of arsenic is 1 ng arsenic/mg hair. Numerous assays were carried out between the 1960s and 2000s, using a variety of methods on hair taken in 1821: results ranged from 4.9 to 38.5 ng/mg. How then can we deny that Napoleon was slowly poisoned by Montholon, who was not only jealous of Napoleon's affair with the Countess de Montholon, but who would have wanted quicker access to the fortune that he would inherit,

19. Kintz Pascal, "Une nouvelle série d'analyse des cheveux de Napoléon confirme une exposition chronique à l'arsenic", *Annales de Toxicologie Analytique*, vol. XIII, no. 4, 2001, pp. 243-246.

and he might have had the complicity of the English, or even the Bourbons!

*

I had carefully reread the work of my predecessors. One fact stood out: Napoleon's hair contained significant quantities of arsenic even before his stay on St. Helena ! For example, 33.4 ng/mg in 1814, according to the 2004 study by Lin et al. Montholon must have started his poisoning attempt very early indeed !

What's more, in order to remove arsenic from the surface of the hair, which is unlikely to come from the bloodstream, the hair analyzed was washed several times with acetone and pure water. However, if the arsenic in the decontamination solution is measured, it was found to be present in negligible quantities, which means that these decontamination solutions are of limited effectiveness, and that much of the external arsenic has remained on the hair's surface[20]. Finally, medical observation of Napoleon reported by physicians does not mention the specific signs of arsenic intoxication: peripheral neuropathy, exfoliative dermatitis

20. STROGI Krystyna, "Hair analysis for monitoring environmental pollution and the resulting human exposure to trace metals: An overview", *Environnement, Risques & Santé*, vol. 5, 2006, p 391-4045.

of the palms and soles, hyperkeratosis, darkening of the skin, and Mees' lines on the nails...

*

I had three of Napoleon's hairs from Vivant Denon's reliquary. They had probably been taken by Marchand in 1821 to make lockets as the Emperor had requested: that is, necklaces, rings, bracelets or rings that members of his family would wear.

Once again, I used the electron microscope and made the following observations, in particular on the hair that had been used to extract the mitochondrial DNA[21]:

1. the hair is straight, light brown and very fine, which corresponds well to the reports by witnesses.
2. they were cleaned with detergents used at the time (soda and black soap) and then decorated (presence of gold and silver) ;
3. a grain of pollen from a type of thistle found on the island is found on a hair ;
4. a mineral grain is present (comprising caesium, lanthanum, neodymium and samarium), indicating the proximity of a volcanic soil ;

21. LUCOTTE Gérard, "Napoléon empoisonné? La fin d'une énigme", *Napoléon 1er*, February, March, April 2013.

5. a small metal fragment from the razor blade is of a composition typical of iron from early 19th-century forges.

*

What did the scanning electron microscope coupled with X-ray microfluorescence show? This technique only detects arsenic above 1 ng/mg.

Figure 3 (see appendix) shows scanning electron microscopy views of Napoleon's and his mother's hair, along with EDX spectra in both cases.

One of the hairs was split lengthwise. The analysis began at the precise point of the cut. The analyzed elements were displayed as a series of peaks, higher or lower depending on the quantity of each element in the hair, This series of peaks showed the presence of carbon, oxygen and sulfur. Sulfur comes from amino acids like cysteine, which form crucial bonds in keratin. *There were no arsenic peaks. There were* identical results at 59 other points on the hair.

I then cut the hair transversely with a razor blade, and repeated the analysis on each cross-section: 117 times. Not the slightest trace of arsenic was found inside Napoleon's hair. Normally, the element passes from the blood into the hair's central medullary canal and then from there, throughout the interior of the hair shaft.

As I also had hair from Madame Mère, Letizia, Napoleon's mother, I repeated the examination using the same method. There was a high arsenic peak on the surface of the hair, visible as crystals, castings or powder. Even inside the hair, the spectrum showed a high peak of this substance. This is an important finding, showing that *arsenic from outside the hair can, over time, penetrate the hair*.

As I wrote in the journal *Napoléon Ier*, and in more detail at the 3rd International Pathography Colloquium in 2009[22], this also explains why there is arsenic inside Napoleon's hair. Using a technology known as *Nano-SIMS*, Kintz had in fact proved, on hair sections from the "Abbé Vignali" batch taken on May 6, 1821, that medulla was highly positive for arsenic; he had incorrectly presumed that this indicated a passage of the toxic agent through the general bloodstream.

At this point, the reader may wonder why my study shows no arsenic in Napoleon's hair, whereas all the other studies detect it, sometimes even at dates when Napoleon was still a general.

*

Here's the solution to the riddle. There are two categories of Napoleon's hair cut after his death.

---

22. Lucotte Gérard, "Pas d'arsenic sur et dans les cheveux de Napoléon", 3rd International Pathography Symposium, April 2009, pp. 259-276.

1. Most of the locks of hair have been treated **with arsenic** for preservation, after being washed and harmoniously arranged under glass.
2. But the hair Marchand collected to make "baskets" was intended to be worn on the skin: it was preserved with copper sulfate, **avoiding arsenic**, whose toxicity was already well known.

There was no arsenic poisoning, nor was there any real motive. Montholon was certainly keen to leave the island, but by 1819-1820, no one had any illusions about the Emperor's failing health Hudson Lowe was satisfied with his position and the salary that went with it. And Lord Bathurst kept a card in his hand... if the Bourbons became a nuisance.

5. Was Napoleon's Body Incorruptible?

Let's "rewind the film" of Joinville and his collaborators' identification of the body. According to Gourgaud[23]:

> *The tips of the feet were white, and it seems that they had come out of the ends of his equestrian boots, the seams of the boots's shafts having rotted... Between the feet, the doctor recognized the silver vases that had been placed there.* (Saint-Denis is more precise: "the heart in a silver saucepan and the stomach in a *timbale* or round sponge box from the Emperor's belongings). *The doctor touched the hands, which looked fine, if a little swollen. The head, with the*

23. GOURGAUD Gaspard, *Le retour des cendres de l'empereur Napoléon*, Arléa, 2003, p. 49.

exception of the nose, which seemed to have been compressed by the top of the coffin, was in perfect condition, only a little swollen. But this only slightly altered his features, and it would have sufficed to have seen the Emperor just once to recognize him at this moment. The doctor lightly touched the flesh of the head and declared it mummified.

Stearin is a fatty acid formerly derived from animal fat, now extracted from palm oil, with similar softening and melting temperatures and a creamy-white appearance. When added to wax, stearin helps candles burn longer, facilitates molding and prevents cracking. Stearin can even replace wax. The stearic aspect referred to by Guillard is therefore reminiscent of candle wax.

On October 15, 1840, the valet de chambre Marchand, who was part of the *La Belle Poule* expedition that returned Napoleon's remains to France, testified:

Dr Guillard, from the frigate, who had omitted none of the precautions involved in the exhumation, took (the headdress) down to the feet and religiously rolled it up to the head, revealing to our astonished eyes the Emperor's perfectly preserved body.

Here is Dr Guillard's report:

The vault having been opened, I descended to the bottom, where the Emperor's coffin rested on a large slab, itself supported by stone uprights. The walls of the vault showed not the slightest trace of dampness... The outer box was closed by long screws, which had to be cut to remove the lid, below was another lead box, closed on all sides, enveloping another perfectly intact mahogany box, and finally a fourth tin box, the lid of which was welded to the walls... The upper limbs were elongated, the forearm and left hand resting on the corresponding thigh, the lower limbs slightly flexed; the slightly elevated head, resting on a cushion, the voluminous skull, the high, broad forehead were covered with hard, sunken, yellowish skin ; so too appeared the outline of the eye sockets, the upper rim of which was lined with eyebrows. Beneath the eyelids were the eyeballs, which had lost little of their volume and shape; these eyelids, completely closed, adhered to the underlying anatomy and were hard to finger pressure, with a few eyelashes still visible at their free edges; the bones of the nose and the tissues covering them were well preserved, with only the lobules and wings having suffered.

The cheeks were puffy, and the skin of this part of the face stood out for its soft, supple, white touch; those of the chin were slightly bluish; this tint was borrowed

from the beard which seemed to have grown after death; as for the chin itself, it showed no alteration and still retained that type proper to the Napoleion's countenance ; the thinned lips were parted, three extremely white incisors could be seen under the upper lip, which was slightly raised on the left.
The hands left nothing to be desired ; nowhere was there the slightest alteration. If the joints had lost their movement, the skin seemed to have retained that primitive color that belongs only to life. The fingers had long, sticky, very white nails. The legs were enclosed in the boots, but the last four toes protruded from each side as a result of broken seems. The skin of these toes was dull white and topped with nails. The anterior region of the thorax was deeply sunken in the middle, ***the belly walls hard and sagging****. The limbs seemed to have retained their shape under the clothes that covered them ; I squeezed the left arm, it was hard and had diminished in volume.*

Now it's Ali's turn:

The first coffin is intact, but damp and even wet at the bottom... When the lid is removed, we see the tin coffin, which is almost completely oxidized, i.e. rust-red... We would have liked to have the two vessels ontaining the heart and stomach, but as these objects are under the legs, and in order to remove them we would have to disturb the legs, which would naturally suffer from being moved, we prefer to leave things as they are... The body is generally in a state of preservation we had not expected.

Emmanuel de Las Cases:

[...] *His two hands especially seemed to belong to someone still breathing, so lively were they in tone and color; one of them, the left hand, was a little higher than the right, and the Grand Marshal, as the coffin was closing, had kissed it and had been unable to return it to its original position... Like a man who had died the day before, so we found the Emperor's body. What had death been doing for twenty years? For twenty years, death had respected his remains.*

Janisch, Hudson Lowe's official secretary:

He was in excellent condition and seemed to have been almost miraculously preserved... the appearance of the whole body was that of someone who had just been buried.

*

So, ten witnesses, present in 1821, saw Napoleon on his deathbed and, in 1840, recognized him: General Bertrand and his son Arthur, the servants Marchand, Saint-Denis dit Ali, Pierron, Archambault and Noverraz, the Englishmen Seale, Janish's father-in-law, and Andrew Darling, and Hodson, nicknamed Hercule. It should be noted that the base of the first coffin was immersed in water, and that the last tin coffin was oxidized. Let's not forget these details.

*

After death, a corpse's skin turns livid, first in the cervical region and then everywhere, within one to two days. Rigidity appears after 6 hours and disappears within 48 hours. As the corpse begins to putrefy, anaerobic bacteria transform proteins into putrescine and cadaverine. The face becomes puffy, subcutaneous phlyctenes form and burst, the body turns green, the head black, and hair, nails and bristles fall out. Four or five years after death, the soft parts have completely disappeared.

The preservation of Napoleon's body is astounding. The absence of skin deterioration, particularly on the hands, is an enigma. Prof. George Bishopric[24], who teaches Anatomic Pathology at at the University of Miami Medical School, answered our questions on this point in writing in 2021: *Here in Florida, at a temperature of 90°F (33° Celsius), in six months the body is reduced to a skeleton. With St. Helena's slightly cooler temperatures and hermetically sealed coffins, I imagine Napoleon's body may have been preserved a bit better. But some twenty years later, the best we could expect was a halloween mask, not a hero's face*[25]*, but we do perform exhumations here, and soft tissues are sometimes reasonably well preserved.* But what chemical preserves bodies and is used for this purpose in taxidermy? Arsenic !

Yes, but it would have required very high concentrations of arsenic, far in excess of any poisoning dosage. Should this be seen as a case of incorruptibility, like certain saints? My colleague Philippe Bornet has suggested this, but he doesn't believe it himself, because Napoleon may have died a Catholic, but he was certainly no saint.

*

There is one last possibility: the formation of an *adipocere?* What is this? Remember what Dr. Guillard said about the "stearic" aspect.

---

24. Personal communication.
25. Bornet Philippe, *Napoléon et Dieu*, Via Romana, 2021, p. 172.

“Adipocere” or cadaver fat is the name given to the transformation of a cadaver’s lipids into a soapy, grayish-whitish substance, soft and greasy to the touch. The decomposition of albumin produces ammonia, which reacts with fats according to the following rule:

$$\text{base} + \text{grease} = \text{soap.}$$

This requires a body rich in fat (Napoleon was overweight), the presence of water (we have seen that the coffin was bathed in humidity) and an absence of oxygen, which was the case under the hermetic tin envelope.

For a corpse will usually putrefy, but it can also:

- mummify in very hot, dry countries, such as the Egyptian desert;
- can be stored at temperatures below -40°C, as in the film *Hibenatus*;
- or transform into adipocere, if the body is buried *in acid soil, submerged or confined to a very small space.* The acidity of marsh peat encourages the formation of adipocere.

“The heart which had been placed in vinegar was placed in a small silver vessel ; the stomach in another one and both were placed in the coffin beside the body,” writes Hudson

Lowe in his May 15, 1821 report to Wellington. Could this vinegar have leaked from the two vases into the coffin?

Adipocere formation is as malodorous as putrefaction. Professor Yves Chatenet, medical examiner at the Poitiers Court of Appeal, writes on this subject[26]:

> *This white coating, especially on the skull and forehead, is reminiscent of the mycelial filaments frequently found inside old coffins, when putrefaction has not been too intense... I note that there is no mention of liquid in the bottom of the coffin and that the clothes are in good condition.*

This would not have been the case had the body putrefied. All this would explain the stearic state noted by Dr. Guillard and the body's apparently miraculous preservation.

I would add that Guillard also notes: "The anterior region of the thorax was deeply depressed in the middle section ; the walls of the belly hard and collapsed". The first part of the sentence is easy to understand, since the heart and stomach were removed, but what about the second? Could it not be that the intestine has been removed? The intestine, and the anaerobic bacteria it contains, are the source of putrefaction. How do we know this? By the testimony of

26. CHATENET Yves (Pr), "Le processus de putréfaction", in ROY-HENRY Bruno, *Napoléon, l'énigme de l'exhumé de Sainte-Hélène*, p. 313.

Prof. René Leriche, who got it from Sir Berkeley Moynihan: at an official reception of the College of Surgeons in 1927, Moynihan took him aside and said:

"Come with me, and I'll show you something rare that nobody else knows about."

He took a key hanging from a chain that opened a safe set into the wall and withdrew an unlabeled glass vial containing a fragment of perforated small intestine.

"It's Napoleon's gut[27]!"

27. Vox Maximilien, *Napoléon*, Le temps qui court, 1959.

6. The Affair of the Masks

How many Napoleonic museums and collectors own a Napoleon mask? Hundreds. Many are copies. Many are fakes, or sometimes copies of the real thing, falsely presented as originals. Don't forget that the only so-called "real" mask is partly a fake.

Chantal Prévost, librarian at the Fondation Napoléon, has endeavored (in three successive versions published in her magazine) to list them, and we thought her work was exhaustive when my colleague Philippe Bornet unearthed yet another mask at the Palais Mamming Museum in Méran, in the Italian Tyrol.

The question of the authenticity of the various masks is complicated and does not lend itself as simple to technical analysis alone. Living history is always complicated. Rather than weary the reader with conflicting dates, types of materials, and testimonials, I will divide this chapter into three parts: authentic masks, probably/partially authentic masks, and obviously fake examples.

I plan to write an entirely separate monograph on the subject of masks.

A/ The authentic mask or Antommarchi mask

Napoleon died on *May 5, 1821* at 5:49 pm.

On *May 6*, witnesses were struck by his beauty: with his slimmed-down, rested features, he resembled the First Consul he had been. Napoleon was indeed very handsome: for proof of this, you need only look at Canova's bust of him in Venice's Correr Museum. Sculptures of history's great and powerful are always flattering, but Napoleon's mother and sisters were also renowned for their beauty.

Madame Bertrand decided it was important to make a cast of this face. But where to find plaster? Andrew Darling, the carpenter-upholsterer, mounted his horse and rode to James Town. No more plaster. All he brought back were statuettes, which had to be crushed. A failure. One of the English doctors, Dr. Burton, knew where on the island to find the gypsum with which plaster is made (I obtained some samples from an area near the airstrip). He ran with Ensign John Ward and a few sailors to George

Island, where they harvested the gypsum by night, by torchlight.

The autopsy had taken place in the meantime ; the gypsum was hastily heated, perhaps with the help of decorator Payne.

On *May 7,* Antommarchi, who had initially recused himself, and Burton set to work. Antommarchi helped Burton, and later claimed that Burton had only helped him.

The Mamluk Ali recounts: "As soon as the public had left, [they] set to work. To facilitate the operation, the Emperor's neck was freed by removing the collar and tie and opening his shirt. Despite the poor quality of the plaster, Antommarchi and Burton fortunately succeeded in pulling the mold first from the face, and then from the other part of the head…".

But the Emperor's features were no longer the same. Bertrand wrote the same day: "We made a plaster cast of the Emperor's face, that was completely disfigured and gave off a very bad smell". The mask's appearance was judged "aged" by Marchand. For this reason, many people refused to believe in the authenticity of the Burton-Antommarchi mask, or suspected that Napoleon's body had been substituted for that of Cipriani. At 7 p.m., the body was placed in the first coffin.

*

Let's digress for a moment and recall a few simple chemistry concepts.

To make plaster, you need gypsum, which is calcined at 150°C and dehydrated before use.

Gypsum is calcium sulfate dihydrate, CaSO4 2H2O, and plaster is sulfate hemihydrate, CaSO4 ½ H2O.

When plaster is hydrated, it can be molded and retains its shape as it dries. When you grind up statuettes called "plaster", you really get gypsum powder, which you can't do anything with, as it can't absorb any more water. This is what Mme Bertrand naively tried at first with the ignorant Antommarchi and the helpful Darling, who was a carpenter and not a mason. This gypsum would have had to be calcined.

In short, plaster is dehydrated gypsum and gypsum is hydrated gypsum. *Strictly speaking,* our wall cladding and some of our statuettes and decorations are made of gypsum (not plaster).

*

Dr. Burton knew all about it. With Hudson Lowe's permission, he had sailed southeast from St. Helena, where he knew he could find gypsum. He brought some back and promptly calcined the gypsum. Alas, the dying man's features, still so beautiful at 8 a.m., had collapsed by 4 p.m.!

With Antommarchi's help, Burton nevertheless made a cast of the face, then a second of the back of the skull. Then he retired, exhausted from his day, leaving the two casts to dry *in situ*. Lieutenant Duncan Darroch of the 20th Regiment wrote in a letter to his mother: "I went in when they were taking the head cast, but the smell was so horrible I couldn't stay. Dr. Burton was taking it with the French doctor.

On *May 8,* Burton returned to make positives. He tried to mold a positive into the negative of the face, but the two remained stuck together. The negative would have had to be broken to save part of the positive's facial block (eyes, nose, mouth and chin). Burton suggested doing nothing more until he returned to England, and leaving everything to the professionals. Everything was left in place.

On *May 9,* Madame Bertrand and Antommarchi steal the facial portion of the mask. When Burton returns for the funeral, he is furious at what he considers a theft. He wrote letters to Madame Bertrand and her husband the Grand Marshal, threatening them with legal action. The French are not entirely wrong, however: there is what we would call today a "right to one's image". In fact, they generously left him the hollow of his skull, which is quite interesting, especially at a time when we believe in Gall's phrenological theories. Grand Marshal Bertrand replied in a letter: "I have seen with gratitude the pains you have taken", but added "you have helped Antommarchi".

But the opposite happened ! Burton jumped at his pen and wrote to London customs to block Bertrand and Antommarchi's luggage on arrival. Arriving in London himself a few days after the French, Burton wanted to have the mask seized by bailiffs. But the English judge declared that he did not have jurisdiction, and accepted General Bertrand's word that the mask was intended for Napoleon's mother.

The cast still intact, Antommarchi, perhaps with the help of the artist Rubidge—but this is only a hypothesis—had completed the central facial mass with a forehead, ears and cranium. The result is an *anastylosis,* as archaeologists sometimes construct them, using stones and materials of a different color from the authentic part. But anastylosis must be reversible and openly acknowledged ; it facilitates the restoration of the monument's antique appearance. Yet Antommarchi has made no admission of this questionable reconstruction.

As for the mold of the back of the skull preserved by Burton, it had been broken by him in a rage. We know this from the widow Ward, who entrusted it to *Sharp's Magazine* in 1853.

*

Let's turn now to the few initial copies authorized by General Bertrand.

Bertrand had a **first copy** of the original cast made, which he kept safe in London, and wrote on September 1, 1821: “This case contains a plaster cast of the Emperor Napoleon’s head made after the mask executed at Longwood by Dr. Antommarchi. Count Bertrand deposited it with Mr. X so that, should the original be lost or broken in transit from London to Rome, a copy could be found. The plaster included in this box can only be disposed of according to Count Bertrand’s order, and in conformity with the intentions that Madame, the Emperor’s mother, will make known to him”. In my opinion, this first copy remained in England and is none other than the RUSI.

A **second copy** was reserved for Canova, the sculptor, to make a marble copy. But Canova never received this copy.

*

As for the **original cast**, where is it? Antommarchi took it with him to the United States and then Cuba, and a century later his family (represented by Gérard Azémar) handed it over to the Musée de la Malmaison, initially as a deposit, before the latter acquired it with its “small skin-covered trunk containing a green box”. According to M. Dancoisne-Martineau, curator of the French domains of St. Helena, this is the first positive print made from Burton’s impression, as analysis of the plaster shows it to be coarse.

*

I examined eight of the historical masks attributed to Napoleon: on the eighth mask, returned from South America and donated by the Azémar family, I took samples in the presence of, and thanks to, Mr. Alain Pougetoux, former curator of the Musée de la Malmaison. A report was drawn up and, following my analysis, the mask became a permanent exhibit at the museum. Figure 6 (see appendix) shows the mask donated by the Azémar family.

It is indeed a transformation of the original mask cast by Antommarchi and Burton on May 7, 1821[28]. Indeed, I found two eyebrow hairs on its surface. One of them had been subjected to a clear lengthwise pull as it passed from the original mold to the positive. Remains of skin and dandruff enabled mtDNA analysis and confirmed the presence of the now famous 16184T mutation typical of the Bonaparte family.

I made a few interesting secondary observations. There were magnesium-rich mineral particles, typical of the lava from the island of Saint Helena. Also present were remnants

28. LUCOTTE Gérard, THOMASSET Thierry, POUGETOUX Alain, "The Napoleon mutation 16184T is that found in the HVS1 sequence of the mtDNA extracted from an eyebrow included in the plaster of the Antommarchi death mask of Napoleon", *International Journal of Sciences*, vol. 4, January 2018, pp. 104-133.

of potassium dichromate, used as a bleaching agent. Last but not least, phosphate particles (characteristic of the island's gypsum).

*

I repeat: the mask on display at Malmaison is, in my opinion, an altered version of Napoleon's original official funeral mask:

- its central part is authentic, made of a coarse plaster (as if made by amateurs) containing an iron-rich aluminosilicate, typical of the island, as well as phosphate;
- and not the peripheral part, made of a much finer plaster of Paris, which Antommarchi found in London[29].

B/ Partially or probably authentic masks

What I mean by "partially authentic" is that the mask was indeed cast on the Emperor's face, but either before his death or without authorization to claim the title of official mask. For, as Major Gideon Gorrequer wrote: "Various attempts at his likeness were made before and after he [Napoleon] was dressed".

29. "Mineralogical and chemical study of the Antommarchi death mask of Napoleon I", *Revue de l'Institut Napoléon*, vol. 214, 2017, p. 27636.

- The **Noverraz 2** mask was offered to the Musée de l'Armée three times, in 1927, 1935 and 1942. The **Noverraz 2** mask does indeed contain Napoleon's hair. I assured the owner, M. Gottardi, a Swiss citizen, that this was the case, and he asked me to appraise it with a view to selling it in the study of M. Coutau-Bégarie, which I was unable to do. It contains a few authentic Napoleonic beard hairs with the mtDNA typical of Letizia's children. My hypothesis is that Noverraz possessed such beard hairs, collected during the funeral cleansing, and had them implanted on the cheeks of the mask by a specialist. Unless he molded the mask for himself, before Marchand shaved the Emperor. Noverraz was very fond of Napoleon: when he knew his master was dying, albeit bedridden and ill, he got up and dressed to see him alive one last time. Figure 4 (see appendix) shows the Noverraz 2 mask.
- The **RUSI** or **Corso** mask. The RUSI is said to have belonged to the collections of the Prince of Essling, and was sold by a certain Louis-Charles de Bourbon to Charles Alder, who gave it in 1953 to the Royal United Service Institution (RUSI), a strategic think-tank set up by Wellington. The curator in possession of the RUSI sold it in 1970, and Forman Piccadilly Limited sold it to the American collector Corso, who disposed of it in 2004 for $13,000. Figure 5 (see appendix) shows the RUSI mask.

I studied this mask, also known as the *Death-Mask of Napoleon*, and the samples taken from it, using face recognition software, light and electron microscopy with X-ray microfluorescence, not to mention mtDNA determination.

The face of the RUSI mask differs from all the others in the puffiness of the skin and the sagging of the flesh, as well as in the rejuvenation of the features due to hypopituitarism—a glandular anomaly—from which he may have suffered[30]. Comparison with a previously unpublished drawing by Marchand shows a total similarity between the two profiles: curvature of the forehead, inter-brow region, bridge and tip of the nose, nostril region, start of the upper lip, flattened on the mask due to its height and the height of the lip.

The quality of the plaster is excellent, especially in the central zone: fine gypsum needles in tight bundles. Electron microscopy with microfluorescence shows fine hairs with 5µ scale rows, typically human. Hair no. 3 has a bulb, allowing us to search for mitochondrial DNA: this hair in fact has the 16184 T mutation.

---

30. FRUGIER Jean-Raymond (Dr), *Napoléon: essai médico-psychologique*, Albatros, 1985.

My opinion, expressed in a recently published article[31], is that RUSI is the copy deposited by Count Bertrand with "M.X".

- The **Baden** mask was apparently cast during the Emperor's lifetime as a gift for the King of Rome, and Antommarchi brought it to Marie-Louise. However, Marie-Louise gave it to her surgeon, Anton Rollet de Baden, in 1830. He was to found the Rollettmuseum, where the mask was housed along with the collection of the phrenologist Gall.
- Another example is the **Borella** mask, named after its owner who tried to sell it to the Musée de l'Armée in 1938.
- The **Hermitage** Mask in St. Petersburg appeared in 2015. It belonged to the son of Eugène de Beauharnais, Napoleon's son-in-law.
- Finally, a papier-mâché mask, Count **Pasolini**'s mask, made from paper washed down with whitewash, was cited by Antommarchi in a speech in New Orleans in 1837. Pasolini is said to have bought it from General Giuseppe Lechi. All I can say in their favor is that they have not yet been proven false.
- Several masks are in South America, in Bogota, Caracas or Santiago de Cuba. These probably include many

31. LUCOTTE Gérard, JULLIEN Frans, THOMASSET Thierry, "The RUSI mask is an authentic replicate of the original death mask of Napoleon", *International Journal of Sciences*, vol. 12, January 2023, pp. 55-68.

masks from the Antommarchi subscription, including, in my opinion, the example from the Archambault collection, the coachman. At best, these are copies of the Antommarchi mask.

Indeed, Antommarchi had other proofs made after 1833 (some claim that he then broke the original, thus committing a crime against history, to enhance the value of the proofs he intended to sell by subscription).

Antommarchi launched a nationwide subscription campaign, complete with leaflets and press inserts. An *ad hoc* committee brought together prestigious names: Bertrand of course, but also Gourgaud, a Murat, a Prince of Moskowa and a Duke of Elchingen. Price of bronze copy: 100 francs. In plaster: 20 francs.

The number of copies made is unknown. Louis-Philippe alone bought 25. Antommarchi eventually sold his reproduction rights to founders Richard and Quesnel in 1834 (later to Susse frères in 1936), and the work was still in the catalog in 1855. The caster, a certain Massimo, was sentenced to eight months in prison for having abused the trust of certain buyers, whom he had led to believe that the copy was the original. In England, Colnaghi & Co was in charge of marketing.

One of the copies was bought by Prince Demidoff, husband of Princess Mathilde, Jérôme's daughter, another passed into Lord Rosebery's collection, another is in the Musée d'Antibes, and yet another in the Musée de l'Armée.

Contemporaries were disappointed by a face that bore so little resemblance to the rest of the iconography. Anatole France described Antommarchi as "Italian, a comedy apothecary, talkative and hungry". Phrenologists, followers of Dr. Gall, did not find Napoleon's genius hump, and for good reason.

C/ List of obviously false masks

- The **Exeter** mask is said to have come from Dr Arnott, who received it from Antommarchi. But why on earth would Antommarchi give a gift to a competitor?
- The **Gilley 1 and 2** masks are believed to have come from Colonel Gilley, the officer on guard duty on St. Helena. However, it is doubtful that he actually stayed on the island, as he does not appear in the list of officers present in 1820, just six months before Napoleon's death. The **Gilley 1** only appeared in 1950, and the **Gilley 2** in 1961. The latter is said to have been a gift from Hudson Lowe's brother. The trouble is, Lowe had only one sister. These two masks are at the Maison Bonaparte in Ajaccio. They are in plaster of Paris, as I have been able to demonstrate, which proves that they are fake, as the plaster available at the time on St. Helena was of mediocre

quality. What's more, how could there be two authentic masks, offered without batting an eyelid by the same person? As absurd as Alphonse Allais's description of Voltaire's skull as a child!

- The **Boys** mask is said to have belonged to the vicar Richard Boys, who returned to England in 1829. It was sold for £170,000, but the Ministry blocked its export. If England believes in it, too bad for them.
- The **Sankey** mask appeared in 1915 and is named after the grandson of Pastor Boys. Proponents of its authenticity maintain that the Burton mask was completed thanks to the painter Rubidge, who drew the Emperor on his deathbed.
- **Noverraz 1** is a plaster mask donated to the Lausanne museum in 1997 by a descendant of Napoleon's servant. If **Noverraz 1** is authentic, then **Noverraz 2** is a fake, and vice versa.
- The **Arnott** mask. Dr. Ganière wrote: "Dr. Arnott assures us that he himself took a wax impression of the imperial face, which was left with the corpse on the night of May 5-6. It would therefore be an authentic, but unofficial, funerary mask.

  Who is Dr. Arnott? He was one of the few English—in fact, Irish—doctors Napoleon accepted at his bedside. The Emperor had noted his keen sense of observation and presented him with a snuffbox. Arnott, whose professional eye was indeed piercing, had noticed Napoleon's tiny variolization scar.

Hudson Lowe had instructed him not to leave Napoleon's body after death. Arnott would therefore have made his cast with modeling wax, not candles, in the absence of Abbé Vignali and the servants. All this was done without authorization, as Arnott left St. Helena in April 1822 without mentioning the casting, which he signed and dated with his thumbprint. Mai is written with an I rather than a Y, as is the case in English, and the word Arnott has only a T, but only for lack of space. The handwriting is similar to that of a letter written to Lowe in September 1821, which is in the Record Office in London as CO 247/32.

*

And now, if you want to understand something, follow me. In 1827, King Jerome became the owner of the cast purchased by his brother-in-law, the King of Württemberg, for £3,000. That same year, it was stolen by a Bavarian, Captain Winneberger, who exhibited it for sale in a London gallery at 454 Oxford Street.

Winneberger is arrested. In 1855, *The Illustrated London News* in April, followed by a book by Watson published in London, reported its existence. Napoleon III decided to pay the £4,000 bail required for Winneberger's release, and recovered the object.

In 1871, did the casket, upholstered in red velvet, escape the flames of the Tuileries fire? In 1895, the American magazine *Mac Clure's magazine New York* published an article by Baron de Saint-Pol, an intimate of Jérôme and Napoleon III, which confirmed this and revealed the whole story.

If the article is to be believed, the mask was probably stolen by an embassy attaché named Schropp, a regular visitor to the Tuileries and familiar to the entire German Gotha, taking advantage of the presence of a Bavarian regiment at the palace. Schropp moved into a private hotel in Nice, but returned to Germany in 1914, leaving the mask to his valet, Combes. When Combes received the order to send the mask to Germany, he hesitated... until 1923. Combes had heard nothing from Baron Schropp (whose intention, we now know, was to donate it to a museum in Nice) and had not received his salary for years. So he entrusted the cast to his friend, the naturalist Rouppert, who exhibited it on rue de l'École de Médecine in Paris.

In July 1923, journalist Henri Simoni wrote: "It can be seen in a store in the École de Médecine in Paris". But it disappeared again in November 1931, only to reappear with another antique dealer, Lucien Ebstein. Combes, ill, asked Ebstein to sell it. In 1929, an American collector, Mr Alfred Pardee, whose wife née Marie-Antoinette Ruelle was French, bought it. His friend, Count Bélénet, was also a friend of Baron Schropp, and remembered perfectly the mask that had appeared on the Baron's mantelpiece. Bélénet gave Pardee his word that it was authentic. The Arnott mask has now left France, but remains the property of Pardee's descendants.

Here are my arguments to say that this mask is false.

1. Arnott died in 1855, and one of his nephews assured us that he himself denied being the author of the mask attributed to him.

2. I studied this mask. It's not made of wax, but of linen cloth covered with plaster mixed with iron filings to give it a pink tone. Wax only makes up the surface layer and is bleached with ceruse and barium sulfate, which prevents browning with age. However, these iron oxide particles were not manufactured until the Industrial Revolution (as early as 1850).

3. In fact, there isn't just one Arnott-type mask, but... five. For example, the one in Munich, whose history resembles that of the previous one: a great name in history arouses the admiration of the potential buyer (that of Emperor Alexander I), a long series of owners makes it possible to muddy the waters and the famous Bavarian captain reappears under the name, no longer of Winneberger, but of Wilneberger. Prof. Stadmuller, who was highly regarded at the time, considered it to be authentic.

7. Was Napoleon French[32]?

The question may come as a shock, but we're not the first to ask it.

"But all in all, you're one of us, you're Italian?" said Louis I, ruler of Etruria, to Napoleon.

"I'm not Italian, I'm French," replied Napoleon forcefully.

At the beginning of the 19th century, the word "Italy" did not correspond to any nation. The peninsula was divided between the Kingdom of Naples in the south, the States of the Holy See in the center and the Kingdom of Piedmont-Sardinia in the north. The rest was scattered between Tuscany, the Milanese region attached to Austria, Venice with its farmland holdings and a few tiny principalities.

32. The attentive reader is referred to the final bibliography containing six articles on Napoleon's Y chromosome haplotype, known as M34, its worldwide distribution, its autosomal profile and the study of some of its descendants.

Italy was obviously part of the Roman Empire, but it was never more than a group of allied or subject cities, subservient to Rome. Even at the end of the Roman Republic, the left bank of the River Po seemed a natural frontier separating Rome's dominions from more or less Celtic territories. Milan, Brescia and Verona were founded by Gauls, and Roman civilization spread there only belatedly, whereas Provence and Languedoc had been firmly anchored to the Roman Republic for centuries. Provençal was thus Latinized long before Milanese or Venetian. We should add that the southern part of the boot was colonized by the Greeks, and that Tuscany, the ancient Etruria, differs profoundly from Lazio.

When Bonaparte led his army across the Alps in 1796, Italy was still only a dream, just as it had appeared to Aeneas' companions fleeing Troy to find a new homeland:

> *Jamque rubescebat stellis aurora fugatis,*
> *Cum procul obscuras colles humilemque videmus Italiam.*
> *Italiam primus conclamat Achates ;*
> *Italiam laeto socii clamore salutant.*
> Already the dawn was reddening, the stars fleeing,
> When we saw the dark hills and flat Italy in the distance.
> Italy!" exclaimed the first Achate;
> Italy!" greeted our companions with a joyful shout...

It was these famous lines from Virgil's Aeneid, Book III, that came back to Napoleon's mind when he dictated the following passage on St. Helena:

"In January [1795] [Napoleon] spent a night on the Col de Tende, from where, at sunrise, he discovered these beautiful plains which were already the object of his meditations. *Italiam! Italiam!*"[33]

Italy was just a dream, but a shared one. "My origin made me considered by all Italians as a compatriot. When Pauline married Prince Borghese, there was only one cry from this family and its allies in Rome and Florence: It's good, it's between us, it's one of our families". At the moment of the coronation, the Italian party prevailed over the Austrian with this consideration of self-love: "After all, it is an Italian family that we are imposing on the barbarians to govern them: we will be avenged of the Gauls".

Napoleon Bonaparte used this dream of unity to his own advantage. Few people know that there was once an Italian Republic, of which Napoleon Bonaparte was the first president before being crowned King of Italy, but it was limited to part of the Po plain. In January 1802, a Constituent Assembly was convened in Lyon, and thirty deputies were elected to designate the President of the Cisalpine Republic. Bonaparte received just one vote in the first round, and Melzi

33. *Commentaires de Napoléon Ier,* Imprimerie impériale, tome 1, p. 66.

twenty-five. Fortunately, Talleyrand intervened and Melzi had the good sense to withdraw; Bonaparte was elected.

*

The next day, the First Consul harangued the crowd and called for the reading of the Constitution of the Republic cis... cisalp...

"Italian, Italian," chants the crowd with irresistible enthusiasm.

"Well, yes, Italian," he says to cheers[34].

Bonaparte was so fond of the new Italy that he annexed Piedmont to it in 1802. Then, in 1805, having received the iron crown of the Lombard kings, he returned to Paris, making a detour via Genoa. In the Doge's palace, he listened favorably to the Doge's speech: "The changes that have taken place... make our isolated existence most unfortunate... Please grant us the happiness of being your subjects". It was a kind of *Anschluss avant la lettre,* as the Genoese, now sovereign of France, annexed his homeland.

The memory of Napoleon Bonaparte, who liberated the city from the Austrians in 1796, is still revered in Milan today, but the Venetians hate him for having put an end to their thousand-year-old republic (they even recently removed

34. FOURNOUX Amable (de), *Napoléon et Venise, L'aigle et le lion,* éditions de Fallois, 2002.

his statue by Canova from the eyes of visitors to the Correr museum), as do the Tyroleans, who have always felt close to the Habsburg empire and have very unpleasant memories of the occupation of their province by its Bavarian allies.

*

If Napoleon wasn't Italian, would he be Corsican? He seems to be, through his father, whose ancestors have been old Ajaccians for generations, but the Bonapartes come from a Tuscan branch that was driven out of Florence during the wars between the Guelphs and the Ghibellines, and settled in Sarzane, on the borders of Tuscany and Liguria, before moving to Ajaccio in the 16th century. Napoleon's father, Charles, in order to get his son into Brienne, had produced titles of nobility linking him to the Bonaparte family of Tuscany, an illustrious family.

Was Napoleon Corsican through his mother, to whom he owed dozens of cousins in Boccognano, while his maternal grandmother was a Pietra-Santa from Sartène? But Letizia, née Ramolino, herself comes from an Italian family, the Counts of Coll'Alto or Collalto, which dates back to the 10th century. The Collalto family, who rival the Capetians in seniority, were, like the Capetians, always sovereign and independent in their lands, and sided with the Emperor against the Pope.

In short, Napoleon was a Corsican of Tuscan origin.

But what about him?

I'm more Champenois than Corsican, because from the age of nine I was raised in Brienne. The French wouldn't have liked it if I'd been surrounded by Corsicans ; on the contrary, I absolutely wanted to be French, even though Corsica, situated between France and Italy, could be the homeland of whoever ruled both. Nevertheless, of all the insults that were hurled at me in so many libels, the one I was most sensitive to was hearing myself called Corsican. Basically, Corsica isn't French, even though it speaks French. I'm not Corsican: I was brought up in France, so I'm French, and so are my brothers... Once in Lyon, a mayor, thinking he was paying me a compliment, said to me: "It's astonishing, Sire, that not being French you love France so much and do so much for her." *It was as if he'd struck me with a stick ! I turned on him... I'm Italian or Tuscan rather than Corsican.*

That paolist (after the pro-independence Pascal Poli, 1725-1807) Corsica that expelled him and his family in 1793. That Corsica which, during the plebiscite conferring the title of Emperor on the First Consul, voted *yes* with only moderate enthusiasm. Even today, when you speak warmly of Napoleon to a Corsican, your interlocutor usually remains politely silent. Didn't Napoleon say of Corsica: "It's a wart on France's nose. If it could be pushed into the depths of the sea, it should be done"?

To sum up: Napoleon claimed to be French, but admitted he was of Tuscan origin and disowned Corsica. Can genetics hold the key to this enigma? The answer lies in the study of Napoleon's Y chromosome haplotype.

*

I had therefore obtained access from the Musée de Châteauroux to Vivant Denon's famous reliquary, which included, in addition to a few hairs, three beard hairs, two of which had a calcified follicle at their base, i.e. cells with a nucleus (which is not the case for red blood cells) and therefore DNA.

DNA is the main component of chromosomes: 23 pairs of chromosomes, each pair comprising one chromosome from the father and the other from the mother. One of these pairs determines sex: XX for female and XY for male. The individual is male because he received the Y chromosome from his father, who received it from his father, and so on in patrilineal order. So much so that the Y chromosome has sometimes been nicknamed Abraham's chromosome. It contains genes that, among other things, cause the development of the testicles.

Like all chromosomes, it's made up of a sequence of genes that can be identified. A kind of license plate. These genes can mutate (change), and the mutation is then characterized by a certain frequency in the general population. A Y chromosome contains certain genes in a certain order, with certain mutations. A haplotype is determined by a first category of genetic markers, corresponding to DNA base substitutions ; a haplogroup is made up of all haplotypes sharing a second category—corresponding to base group repeats—of genetic markers. Certain haplotypes are more frequent in certain ethnic groups and regions of the world than in others, and thus form haplogroups.

Now, as we shall see, on the part of the Y chromosome that recombines with the X, a haplotype known as *E1b1b1c1* is determined (see figure 7 in appendix), which will act as the touchstone for the genetic identification of male members of the Bonaparte family.

But how to obtain this haplotype from a hair follicle? First, I used an electron microscope equipped with an X-ray generator to examine my precious beard hairs. A beam of X-rays can be directed at any point on the specimen under observation, giving the corresponding atomic spectrum. This examination revealed, at the base of two hairs (out of the three in my possession), a zone rich in calcium and phosphate, probably containing organic tissue and therefore DNA.

On observation, these hairs were indeed beard hairs, for:

- they were larger in diameter than the hair;

- their cross-section was angular due to the razor's forceful passage, which inclined them;
- the rows of scales were very close together, indicating rapid growth.

At the base of the hairs, I noted traces of beard soap and small pieces of industrial steel (rich in chromium and manganese) from the razor, *blood cells* and dried horny tissue corresponding to the follicular sheath surrounding the hair bulb.

These calcium- and phosphate-rich zones were isolated and incubated at a suitable temperature, before being immersed in a lysing solution (i.e. one that destroys cell membranes, allowing DNA extraction). Standard precautions were taken to avoid contaminating the sample with the technician's DNA (gloves, masks). The PCR technique was then used to duplicate the DNA found until a sufficient number of molecules had been obtained[35]. Napoleon's

35. LUCOTTE Gérard, THOMASSET Thierry, HRECHDAKIAN Peter, "Haplogroup of the Y Chromosome of Napoleon the first", *Journal of Molecular Biology Research*, vol. 1, no. 1, December 2011, pp. 12-19. The genetic markers used in this study were SNPs (single nucleotide polymorphisms), which were already known in the scientific literature. After determining that the DNA extracted from the follicles did indeed contain a Y chromosome, the successive use of 10 SNPs:- M125, M174, M35, M33, M123, M81 and M78, to identify the main branches, - then M34, M84 and M290 to determine terminal differentiation, made it possible to specify that the haplogroup was E1b1b1c1, - M3 being the ultimate marker.

haplotype could thus be determined using the first category of markers.

*

Prince Napoleon, a descendant of Napoleon's brother Jérôme (his Y chromosome should therefore be the same as that of Napoleon Bonaparte and his father Carlo Bonaparte), was happy to take a mouth swab for comparison. This required a certain amount of courage, as I might have discovered that his historical lineage was in fact illegitimate. But no, Charles Bonaparte, born in 1950, is a fourth-generation descendant of Jérôme Bonaparte, Napoleon's youngest brother and King of Westphalia. This smear was used to establish what is known as his Y-STR profile (based on so-called microsatellite markers), made up in this case of 37 genetic markers. All that remained was to compare the two haplotypes: that determined from the hair and that of Charles (see figure 8 in appendix).

They were **identical for 3 key markers** (DYS19, DYSICAIIa and DYSICAIIb determined in Napoleon) and included in Charles those of haplogroup E1b1b1c1, whose final differentiation marker is E-M34 (as well as M84 and M290 absent).

*

Where is E-M34 found? In Southern Europe and North Africa; its frequency rises to 6.6% in Sicily. It is also common in Ethiopia and the Near East.

It is divided into subgroups: subgroup A among German and Spanish populations, B among Arab populations around the Persian Gulf, C made up of British and Irish, D1 among Ashkenazi Jews and D2 in the Near East and Turkey.

It is possible to date the age of these five haplogroups, as mutations inevitably occur, and their number is proportional to their duration: 3,850 years. The European subgroup would be 3,525 years old. Migration to Europe would therefore have occurred from Middle Eastern populations (Lebanon, Syria, Palestine and Turkey) present since the 5th millennium BC. The Napoleonic haplotype was present on the shores of the Dead Sea in present-day Jordan ; it conquered the southeast and northwest of present-day Turkey, moved into Greece and the Balkans, and from there reached Sicily and Calabria, Naples, Sarzane and Ajaccio[36].

36. LUCOTTE Gérard, DIÉTERLEN Florent, "Frequencies of M34, the Ultimate Genetic Marker of the terminal differenciation of the Napoleon the First's Y Chromosome Haplogroup E1b1b1c1, in Europe, Northern Africa and the Near Est", *International Journal of Anthropology*, 2014, vol. 29, no. 1-2, pp. 27-41.

Figures 9 and 10 in the appendix show the frequencies of M13 (the terminal SNP marker of differentiation) in the Middle East, mainland Italy, Sicily, Sardinia and Corsica.

*

We know that Napoleon's paternal ancestors, known down to the 17th generation, include Guglielmo Bonaparte, who lived in Sarzane in the 13th century, and his distant descendant Giovanni Bonaparte, who lived in the 15th century and settled in Ajaccio. Nine more generations and we end up with Carlo Bonaparte, father of Napoleon.

Figure 11 (appended) shows Napoleon's paternal ancestry over 17 generations.

Like any self-respecting aristocrat, Napoleon knew his ancestors inside out. He once confided to Dr. Antommarchi, his last physician:

"My most ancient ancestor, who lived in Tuscany, had the same political principles that I profess today."

In other words, he was a Ghibelline, a supporter of the emperor against the pope, a supporter of the Holy Roman Empire, a federalist and unifier of all of those ancient cities that were as jealous of their independence from the Empire as they were of Rome's, and a fighter for imperial authority.

"What does Your Highness think of all this," I asked Prince Napoleon.

"I'm not at all surprised, my dear Professor. Do you know what Francesco Bonaparte's nickname was?"

"Giovanni's son, who had the first contact with Corsica? A mercenary in the service of the Republic of Genoa?"

"Himself. He was nicknamed... 'Le Maure de Sarzane.'"

Here's another way of understanding the Corsican flag: the Moor is not only the age-old enemy who ravages Corsica's coasts, but sometimes, also the one who takes root there.

*

Napoleon's ancestors came from the distant East, which gave birth to such great conquerors as Alexander, Artaxerxes, Mohammed and others... Does this explain his fascination with Egypt? His plan to enter the service of the Grand Turk before Vendémiaire 13? His conquest of Malta?

Neither totally Italian nor completely French, Napoleon was naturally destined to rule both nations, and to replace the Germanic emperors in whose service his Ghibelline ancestors had so often placed themselves. Girding the iron crown of the Lombards, replacing the Habsburgs, seizing their title of King of the Romans, marrying their daughter and making all the subjects of Europe his vassals, including the countries of the Confederation of the Rhine: this was the program of the new Charlemagne.

This conquering temperament and his preference for empire are rooted in deeply in his origins. Jean-Claude Valla[37] understood this well:

> *Time and again, Napoleon has posed as the successor to Charlemagne... Yet it is this nostalgia for the empire that helps us understand the Napoleonic adventure... An unworthy son of the Enlightenment, Napoleon made use of the utopias of 1789 before riding over these myths to their complete abnegation.*

In *Le Grand Empire*, Jean Tulard[38] confirms: "The link that binds the non-annexed but dependent countries to the Emperor is neither federal nor federative, but simply vassal-like: the Emperor is the suzerain of the kings of Europe. The family system fits seamlessly into this Carolingian conception of the Empire."

---

37. VALLA Jean-Claude, *La nostalgie de l'Empire, une relecture de l'histoire napoléonienne*, Dualpha, 2004.
38. TULARD Jean, *Le Grand Empire*, Albin Michel, 1982.

8. Who Are the Descendants of Marie Walewska?

Deciphering Napoleon's mtDNA was a good start, but could we also tackle the Y chromosome and draw conclusions about his descendants other than Charles? This chromosome makes it possible to certify family and dynastic filiations, whatever the uncertainties (don't you agree, ladies!) of civil status.

Take, for example, Marie Walewska, "Napoleon's Polish wife". Marie Walewska was born in 1786 into a Polish noble family. Marie's father, who had joined the Polish Legions, had taken part in the 1794 uprising against Russia. But this led to the third partition of Poland in 1795, and he died of grief and wounds. His widowed mother hired a French tutor to bring up her daughter, Nicolas Chopin, the musician's father. At the age of 14, she entered the Convent of Our Lady of the Assumption in Warsaw, where she received a good family education. At 17, she married Count Walewski of an illustrious family, a chamberlain in his seventies, and had a son. Marie was beautiful, gentle and modest.

In 1806, Napoleon occupies Poland. Marie is twenty and appears at a ball organized by Talleyrand. She danced with the Emperor. The next day, Napoleon sent her a gigantic bouquet of flowers with a letter: "I have only seen you, I have only admired you, I only desire you". The whole of Warsaw soon heard about it. Many Polish patriots thought she should take advantage of the situation to plead Poland's cause. Even her husband turned a blind eye as Marie sacrifices herself to Moloch.

The two lovers spent three months together at Finckenstein Castle. It seems they were very much in love with each other. Marie pleaded for her fatherland, but Napoleon gently resisted, agreeing only to found a Grand Duchy of Warsaw. Alexander was born of their love affair. On May 4, 1810; he was to become Napoleon III's Minister of Foreign Affairs. He was legally recognized by Count Walewski as his son, and Napoleon, his biological father made him a count, endowing his mother with a large fortune. Although a Catholic, Marie divorced her debt-ridden husband to protect her son's fortune. She considered herself his lawful wife until his death, after which Marie settled near Paris in 1813. In 1814, she visited Napoleon on Elba. Finally, she married Count d'Ornano, a distant cousin of Napoleon. She died at the age of 31, of toxemia in her last pregnancy.

In her *Memoirs,* she describes her affair with Napoleon as "a sacrifice made to her country".

At Père-Lachaise cemetery, an urn still contains her heart.

*

Napoleon's son, Count Alexander Walewski, became a Second Empire celebrity. He also had a famous mistress, the tragedienne Rachel Félix.

Born in 1821 to a couple of Alsatian Jewish peddlers, Rachel moved to Paris with her parents, and as a child of the street markets, she was accustomed to acting and dancing in front of the crowds for tips. She entered the French Theatre at the age of 17. One of her first roles was that of Camille in Corneille's *Horace*. It was a triumph. The whimsical Rachel became rich and famous.

The handsome Prince de Joinville, the same man who was to retrieve Napoleon's remains in 1840, sent her a letter in which he had written the words "Where, when, how much?", to which she replied: "Tonight, at my place, free of charge".

Count Walewski later became her regular lover. One evening, arriving at her apartment unexpectedly early, his coat rain-soaked and cold, he took it off himself and put it to dry in a closet. Later, expecting it to have dried out, he went to get it himself himself and, on opening the coat closet, found, a hussar!

Count Walewski is said to have fathered another Alexander, born in 1844. Rachel died of tuberculosis at just 36, an unhappy, romantic end befitting a tragedienne. She was indisputably a role model for Sarah Bernhardt. Her body lies in the Jewish section of Père-Lachaise.

From Alexandre onwards, the French Walewski line culminates in the present-day Count Alexandre Colonna Walewski. For three generations, the French Walewskis have been involved in the mechanical and steel industries. Today, the Count has passed on his company to his sons, Touax SCA, a Euronext-listed company specializing in the rental and management of logistics equipment such as containers, valued at 55 million euros.

A few years ago, Count Walewski was refused registration of his title with the Seal of France, an administrative act that guarantees against usurpation. To his great disappointment, despite an appeal, the Conseil d'État (in 2012) ruled against him, using the 1812 Civil Code as a basis, on the grounds that his ancestor, Rachel's lover, had only had one natural child. The Count, incensed, protested that his ancestor Alexandre Antoine Walewski, had been recognized, albeit belatedly, but to no avail. He was still reeling from disappointment when I met him and he invited me to his home.

*

The Count was immediately interested in my early work, which he had heard about earlier. Demonstrating discretion (and prudence, he had made careful inquiries about me), he received me and his wife in his Neuilly apartment with truly charming simplicity. Probably justifiably annoyed by questioning of the title inherited from his glorious ancestor, he saw it as a means to genetically establish his ancestry. I learned from him about the French Walewskis, who have little in common with the Polish Walewskis. The Count keeps a blog on the subject[39]. The French branch is made up of the kind of captains of industry the Second Empire knew so many of.

I then showed that Charles Bonaparte and Count Walewski shared virtually the same haplogroup. By comparing the Y chromosomes of two distant cousins who share the same ancestor, Carlo Bonaparte (Napoleon's father), without sharing the same political options, I set myself a dual goal: to establish the Walewski parentage, as Rachel's sexual excesses were causing us some concern, and to attempt to reconstitute the Y-STR markers of Napoleon I's Y chromosome.

39. colonnawalewski.ch

I renamed my two subjects CN and ACW, for Charles Napoléon and Alexandre Colonna Walewski. Two of history's great names reduced to number-plate initials: Science has no respect for anything!

By examining the non-recombinant part of their Y chromosome, I was able to study around a hundred Y-STRs (*Y-short tandem repeats*)[40]. These sequences are formed by the repetition on the chromosome of identical motifs, generally 2 to 4 nucleotides long.

Microsatellite sequences can exist in different allelic forms: we've already seen this in the Charles-Napoléon Y-STR profile. These different allelic values are characterized by numbers corresponding to the number of repeats of identical motifs: a kind of DNA stuttering!

As a reminder of what a gene allele is, I'll take a well-known example, that of ABO blood groups, determined by a gene on chromosome 9. This gene can take the form of the A allele or the B allele, resulting in the formation on the surface of the red blood cell of antigenic markers known as A, B or none, which are then labelled O. One of the two alleles comes from the father, the other from the mother. If the alleles are A/A or A/O, the blood group will be A. If the alleles are B/B or B/O, the blood group will be B. If the

40. LUCOTTE Gérard, MACÉ Jacques, HRECHDAKIAN Peter, "Reconstruction of the Lineage Y Chromosome Haplotype of Napoleon the First", *International Journal of Sciences*, September 2013, vol. 2(9), p. 127-139.

alleles are A/B, the blood type will be AB, and if the alleles are neither A nor B, the blood type will be O.

*

However, microsatellite sequences have similar allelic values in CN and ACW in 131 cases and different values in only 6 cases.

Conclusion: Charles Napoleon and Alexandre Colonna Walewski are too similar not to have a common ancestor. Rachel didn't cheat on her lover, and Count Walewski is a descendant of Napoleon. Although his ancestry includes two natural children, he has every moral right to bear the title of Count that the Emperor bestowed on his ancestor.

And we celebrated this good news by drinking orange juice poured from the countess's own hands. By comparing the 133 allelic values of the microsatellite sequences between CN and ACW, it was possible to infer those of Napoleon, of which only 3 were previously known.

*

Alexandre's piercing blue gaze during our talks prompted me to later undertake a new study on a lock of Napoleon's hair collected in 1811, provided by the renowned Belgian collector Pierre d'Harville (an eminent

Napoleon I specialist for over thirty years). From the dandruff covering this hair, I proceeded to study the gene that codes for eye color and those that determine hair and skin color[41]. Dandruff is not a skin cell, but a large cell whose proliferation is caused by bacteria. More DNA can be extracted from their nuclei than from the hair itself, making it possible to study other genes[42].

Napoleon's skin was white, his eyes light (blue or rather light blue) and his hair blond to red (see figures 12 and 13 in appendix). This freckling is already visible under light microscopy. The hair on the 1811 lock is reddish and fine, averaging 55 μ in diameter.

*

I spoke to Nicole Garnier, curator of the Musée Condé in Chantilly, about Napoleon's physical appearance, which many people imagine as a Mediterranean-type Corsican with brown eyes, dark hair and a swarthy complexion. The most interesting painting, from the point of view of

---

41. LUCOTTE Gérard, MACÉ Jacques, THOMASSET Thierry, "Napoleon the First, a Corsican with pale skin, clear eyes and red hair: DNA evidence for these phenotypic traits", *International Journal of Sciences*, vol. 10, July 2021, pp. 1-5.
42. LUCOTTE Gérard, BOUIN WILKINSON Alexandra, "An autosomal STR profile of Napoleon the First", *Open journal of Genetics*, vol. 4, 2014, p. 292-299.

historical accuracy, is that by François Gérard, painted in 1803 from life according to Nicole Garnier: the First Consul is pale with blue eyes and reddish hair (see figure 14 in appendix). Denis Davydov, who met him at Tilsit in 1807, and Lord Lyttleton, in 1815, attested to this reddish hue.

Napoleon probably used dye to darken his hair and soften its freckles. Towards the end of his life on St. Helena, he neglected himself and no longer dyed his hair, hence some English caricatures of him as a redhead.

9. Descendants of Lucien Bonaparte in the United States !

Do you know Peter Hrechdakian? Probably not. But he's well known in the Armenian community. This fertilizer producer presides over the destiny of Brussels-based Unifert Group SA. Hrechdakian is passionate about Armenian history and traditions. It was he who put me on the trail of Mike Clovis [43] [44] [45].

---

43. LUCOTTE Gérard, MACÉ Jacques, HRECHDAKIAN Peter, "Reconstruction of the Lineage Y Chromosome Haplotype of Napoleon the First", *International Journal of Sciences*, vol. 2(9), September 2013, pp. 127-139.
44. LUCOTTE Gérard, HRECHDAKIAN Peter, "New Advances Reconstructing the Y Chromosome Haplotype of Napoleon the First based on three of his living descendants", *Journal of Molecular Biology Research*, vol. 5(1), 2015, pp. 1-10.
45. LUCOTTE Gérard, HRECHDAKIAN Peter, SAVARD Denis, "Towards a full-length Y-Chromosome DNA Sequence of Napoléon the First: beyond the E-M34 SNP subhaplogroup", *Austin journal of genetics and genomic research*, vol. 2(2), 2015, p. 1-4.

Mike Clovis is an American citizen. He is the fifth descendant of Lucien Bonaparte, Napoleon's younger brother. Lucien, six years younger than Napoleon, shared his older brother's passion for politics. Lucien was uncontrollable: in 1794, he had married the daughter of his innkeeper, Christine Boyer, without his family's permission. His role in the success of the day of 18 Brumaire was decisive: he presided over the Conseil des Cinq-Cents. He became Minister of the Interior in 1799, and was widowed in 1800. One of his main missions in 1799 was to falsify the results of the plebiscite on the constitution of Year VIII. Lucien was appointed ambassador to Spain, a mission in which he did not always comply with his instructions. As his brother was childless, he believed himself entitled to succeed him, especially on a throne he had helped him conquer. In 1803, he married Alexandrine Jacob de Bleschamp, even though Napoleon wanted him to marry the Queen of Etruria. He left Paris in 1804, after a stormy last exchange with his brother. In 1807, he refused to divorce his wife. Attempting to reach America, he was arrested by the English, who held him for three years. In 1814, he returned to Rome, where the Pope made him Prince of Canino. In 1815, he reconciled with Napoleon *in extremis* and proposed a dictatorship of public salvation. With the failure that we know.

From his first marriage, Lucien had only daughters, and the second was very prolific; he had, among others,

Louis-Lucien born in 1813, in Thorngrowe, England. The *Dictionnaire Napoléon* indicates that he married the daughter of sculptor Cecchi in 1833, and that they separated in 1850 without issue.

Well, it's not true! Louis-Lucien Bonaparte's son was Louis Clavering Bonaparte (1859-1894), father of Valentine (!?) Clavering George Clovis (1883-1979), father of Cyril Abel Clovis (1925-2009), father of Mike Clovis born in 1948.

Our study shows that the Y-STRs profile of Mike Clovis (MK) shares 93 allelic values with those of CN and ACW, 7 values differ[46].

*

Are there any men with a Y chromosome resembling Napoleon's in Sarzane, Italy[47]? Sarzane, on the banks of the Magra near La Spezia, as we have seen, is the birthplace of the Bonapartes. However, a study of the distribution of SNP markers in Italy, carried out by my colleague Marco Grappi, has shown that there are three individuals in this region identified as M34. Carrying the M34 marker means being related

46. The DNA study of the 1811 wick films identified 18 allelic values in Napoleon's Y-STRs profile. Line-specific markers appeared: DYS545 for Jérôme, DYS442 for Lucien and DYS712 and DYS481 for Napoléon, depending on the direct line studied in Alexandre Walewski.
47. Lucotte Gérard, Grassi Marco, "Sarzane et le profil ADN de Napoléon", *Napoléon Ier*, special issue no. 31, December 2019, pp. 89-95.

in some way to Napoleon. One of them, Abbé *Cipollini,* whose ancestry could be traced back fifteen generations, was compared with Mike Clovis, Charles Napoléon and Alexandre Colonna Walewski (see figure 15 in appendix). The homology percentage with Mike Clovis is 88.7% for 106 markers. The same applies to *J.Pennuci* and *A.Arrighi:* 83.8% and 75% homology with Mike Clovis, but on only 37 markers.

These three Italian subjects are therefore descended from families allied to those of Bonaparte. However, we know for a fact that at the beginning of the 16th century, around one hundred families, mainly from Sarzane, were sent from the mainland to populate Ajaccio[48].

48. Back in 2013, the American firm Family Tree DNA (ftDNA), with which I regularly collaborate, proposed a technology consisting of sequencing the entire DNA of the Y chromosome. This technology was used for Mike Clovis' Y chromosome.It is listed in the corresponding database under the acronym E-PH3893. A total of 55.25% of its chromosome sequence was obtained here, and the number of allelic values at the STRs markers in its profile was determined for a total of 491 markers. All SNP variants and allelic values of the Y-STRs profile determined in my previous studies were confirmed. First, Mike Clovis' Y chromosome sequence was compared with those of four other individuals (already in the bank, with similar Y sequences). The comparison then focused on the Y chromosome sequences of Mike Clovis and Carlo Cipollini. Their sequences, designated YF03109 and Y-F11420 respectively, belong to the same group as E-PH3893, which includes two other individuals— an Armenian and a Russian—who have since been studied). MikeClovis and Carlo Cipollini share mutations Y59556, Y 58897 and BY36877/Y135092, plus 5 additional SNPs. A summary of these determinations is given above.It is possible to estimate the date of origin of the common lineage between Mike Clovis and C.Cipollini at 2,900 years. Mike Clovis and C.Cipollini's closest common ancestors lived around 1,050 years ago.

In France, the peak frequency of the M34 marker in my own study of 111 individuals in Ajaccio was 8.1%.

Sitting on the terrace of the Grand Café in Ajaccio, when you've seen twelve people pass by, one of them is related to Napoleon.

10. Was Napoleon III his Father's Son? Was he his Uncle's Nephew?

Let's take a look at the future Napoleon III, born in 1808 to Louis Bonaparte, King of Holland, and Hortense de Beauharnais. The delivery by two renowned doctors of the time, Baudelocque and Corvisart, was followed by a certificate stating that the child had been born prematurely. Less than nine months earlier, Louis and Hortense had met again in Toulouse, and Hortense had written to her brother that she had become pregnant on that date.

This birth gave rise to many rumors at the time, and doubts were cast on the legitimacy of Louis Bonaparte's parentage. Jérôme, the uncle of the future Napoleon III, once told him:

"You're no Bonaparte."

He replied with cold humor:

"Yes, I do. I have his family."

Yet his father Louis had little doubt about his paternity, and wrote in his will: "I leave all my inheritance to my universal heir, Louis-Napoléon, the only son I have left".

*

I will now present a work that was the subject of a lecture I gave at *Les Invalides*, to representatives of the Souvenir napoléonien, and was later the subject of a much-cited article in *Le Figaro*[49].

When I studied dandruff from a lock of Napoleon III's hair supplied by Pierre d'Harville and taken after Sedan, during his captivity, I found neither the haplotype nor the haplogroup of Napoleon I already described, but another haplotype[50], typically Corso-Sardinian: haplotype XII. I found this haplotype in the dandruff of another lock of hair of Prince Eugène, son of Napoleon III, also supplied by Pierre d'Harville. It concerns 40% of Corsicans: 36 individuals out of 89 in the Corte region.

Paradoxically, Napoleon III has a Corsican Y haplotype, while Napoleon I has a Middle Eastern one.

---

49. MALLEVOÜE Delphine (de), "Et si Napoléon III n'était pas le neveu de l'Empereur?", *Le Figaro*, April 25, 2014.
50. LUCOTTE Gérard, PINNA Antoine, MERCIER Géraldine, "Haplotypes du chromosome Y en Corse", *Comptes rendus Biologies*, Académie des Sciences, vol. 325, 2002, p. 191-196.

Dilemma: how to explain that Napoleon I is not the uncle of Napoleon III? Either King Louis is not Napoleon III's biological father, or Louis' father is not Letizia's husband Carlo. Either Hortense cheated on her husband or Letizia cheated on hers.

In order to make a decision, Louis' haplotype had to be determined, and a sample taken from his body. Louis died on July 25, 1846 in Livorno. His body and that of his son Napoléon-Louis (who died in Forli in 1831) were repatriated from Italy, and lie next to Carlo Bonaparte, father of Napoléon Ier, and Napoléon-Charles, Louis' first son who died young in 1807, in the Saint-Leu-Saint-Gilles church in Saint-Leu-la-Forêt, named Saint-Leu-Taverny until 1915.

Jacques Macé, then president of the *Souvenir napoléonien,* submitted a request to the municipal authorities, but received no positive response. We are therefore reduced to conjecture.

Haplotype XII is highly specific to a geographical area. Louis' father was probably a Corsican from the island. Where would Hortense have met him?

In her *Memoirs,* Hortense is candid. On the subject of the Toulouse reunion, she confided on August 22 to her brother, to whom she told everything:

> *I'm with the king together. I don't know if it will last. I hope so, because he wants to be better for me, and*

you know I've done nothing to be bad. Finally, Louis bears no resemblance to his brothers.

These are the three reasons why I opt for the other Solution: that Napoleon III is indeed Louis' son (which many doubted during the Second Empire), but that Louis is only Napoleon's half-brother. Their only common ancestor was Letizia Ramolino. It was she who had an illegitimate child, not Queen Hortense.

Letizia's reputation as a woman of duty is a little dented, but historical truth has its place. As Leonardo da Vinci said: "The truth is always better, however thin it may be".

*

Can we assume that Louis' father is Marbeuf, the island's governor? Didn't Letizia take Marbeuf's portrait with her when she was expelled from Corsica in 1793? I don't think so: Louis, Charles, René de Marbeuf was Breton. Napoleon did have blond hair tending towards red, as seen in a painting by Bacler d'Albe and in one by Gérard, but this was due to a mutation in the MC1R gene called D294 H. However, the Celtic population (in Ireland, for example), when they have red hair, generally carry another mutation called R160W.

11. Has the Emperor been Emasculated?

Among Antommarchi's belongings were some of Napoleon's bodily remains ; for a doctor, these are interesting anatomopathological specimens, for Napoleon's companions in misfortune, they were relics. One of them, with liturgical ornaments and a bequest of 100,000 F, went to Abbé Vignali. Napoleon was very fond of this rough-hewn Corsican priest. Vignali was a medical doctor, which is why Antommarchi took him on as his secretary during the autopsy.

Here's what the Mamluk Ali says in his *Memoirs:* "The sheet on which the operation had just been performed was stained with blood in many places ; it was cut by most of those present and each had a piece, the English taking most of it". This is an interesting remark: it shows that all those present were aware that they were living through a historic moment, and wished to keep a relic of the event.

"Before sewing up the body, Antommarchi, seizing the moment when English eyes were not fixed on the corpse, had extracted two small pieces from a rib, which he gave to Vignali and Coursault"[51]. In so doing, Antommarchi was giving a relic to Abbé Vignali, in recognition of the trouble he had taken to set up the secretariat.

This anatomopathological fragment remained in the Vignali family until 1916, when it was sold to the English antiquarian Maggs Bros. In 1924, it became the property of the American collector Abraham Simon Wolf Rosenbach (1876-1952), for £400. Rosenbach had bought it as a "mummified tendon taken from Napoleon's body during the autopsy", based on the text by Louis-Étienne Saint-Denis (1788-1856), known as Mamelouk Ali.

*

In 1927, the piece was exhibited at the Museum of French Art in New York. Strangely enough, rumors began to circulate that it was a penis, and the exhibition was a great success with the female public, who, as the press of the time would have it, found it hard to stifle their giggles. It was sold to the bibliophile Donald Frizell Hyde (1909-1966), then to Rosenbach's successors, before passing into

51. Mamelouk Ali, "Mémoires", *Revue des Deux Mondes*, September 1921, p. 640.

the hands of the collector Bruce Gilmeson, who tried to sell it in 1972. It was not until October 26, 1977, however, that it was acquired for $3,000 at Drouot by the American urologist John Kingsley Lattimer.

*

Lattimer had a passion for military and historical memorabilia. He had been in charge of the health of the war criminals tried at Nuremberg in 1946, and had kept some of the ropes of famous hangmen. In 1963, he had also taken part in the Kennedy assassination inquiry and kept a piece of the fabric from the car in which the American president had collapsed. Lattimer used to tell friends that Antommarchi had taken revenge for Napoleon's mistreatment of him because he thought his service was bad. He lived in Englewood, New Jersey, and carefully hid the relic under his bed, in a box lined with blue velvet, topped with a lid bearing a crowned N. He claimed that he had examined it with a CT scanner, that X-rays had confirmed that it was indeed a penis, and that he was determined to prove it, should the French government allow him to go to *Les Invalides* to check whether Napoleon's body was missing anything. How can you not believe a professor of urology at Columbia University? Personally, I fail to see what interesting information a CT scan can provide on soft tissue, and what information X-rays can give us in terms of histological analysis. In 2016, the piece was resold by his daughter to a "mysterious Argentinian buyer", which was noted by *Le Quotidien du Médecin* in one of its June 23 articles.

*

This mysterious "Argentinian", in fact a Colombian, was Mr. B. Cao, a museum director acting on behalf of Mr. Sou Mong, a Chinese millionaire with an American passport. Mr. Sou Mong had signed a check with enough figures to overcome the reluctance of Professor Lattimer's daughter. Then, fully informed of my work (in 2018), he wished to contact me. One question nagged at him: was the piece in the Vignali collection genuine? Was it a penis? Had someone dared to emasculate the greatest strategist of all time, the master of the world, the man Clausewitz had called "the god of war himself"?

*

The "penis" was arranged in a handsome two-compartment box (figure 16 in appendix), with a gold-crowned N, made by Sangorski & Sutcliffe: in one compartment, the anatomopathological specimen, in the other two envelopes containing what appeared to be hairs, which I later had the opportunity to study. Mr. B. Cao sent me three fragments of the so-called penis (figure 17 in appendix) for analysis.

First, I carried out an examination using a scanning electron microscope, capable of using X-rays to analyze the atomic spectrum of the image point by point. At the same time, I extracted the DNA and amplified it by PCR. The product was purified on agarose gel and sequenced (for the hypervariable 1 region of mitochondrial DNA). These samples showed longitudinal striations, typical of muscle cells (see figure 18 in appendix). They were rich in calcium and phosphorus (see appendix figure 19). They were therefore cartilage or tendon, not penis. Sequencing also revealed the characteristic 16184T mutation in fragments A and B. In conclusion, an authentic remnant of the Emperor, but a tendon and not a penis.

Vignali had inherited these relics and his sister's descendant had sold them in 1916. The Maggs Bros catalog described it as "a mummified tendon"; and that was the truth. Another sample returned to Coursault and is now in the Musée de la Malmaison in a glass cylinder, which I was able to examine and photograph.

My article on the subject appeared in 2022[52] and Mr. Sou Mong was very pleased with the results of my work. I saw

52. LUCOTTE Gérard, BORENSZTAJN Stéphan, "SEM-EDX and mtDNA analyses of the penis of Napoleon", *International Journal of Sciences*, vol. 11(5), May 2022, pp. 15-21.

him in person in Paris in March 2023; I believe he is interested in producing a documentary film about Napoleon.

I had used both samples for DNA analysis. I still had the third, which I was going to devote to a new study. It was to overturn everything we knew for sure about the causes of Napoleon's death.

12. Was Napoleon Exiled to an Unhealthy Land with the Intention of Killing him?

First, we need to examine whether the island of St. Helena was unhealthy in the early 19th century.

Dr. Barry E. O'Méara explained this in his *Relation des événements arrivé à Sainte-Hélène postérieure à la nomination de Sir Hudson Lowe au gouvernement de cette île,* published in Paris in its French translation as early as 1819.

But who is this O'Meara? Born in 1786, and therefore aged thirty-three in 1819, O'Meara was assistant surgeon to the 62nd Infantry Regiment, then surgeon on the *Bellérophon* that took Napoleon to St. Helena. Attached as physician to Longwood, he was bullied by Hudson Lowe over the Emperor's health reports, which the governor wanted to control, and left the island on August 2, 1818. His will reads:

"I take this opportunity of declaring that, with the exception of a few trifling and unintentional errors in *The Voice from Sainte-Helena*, the book is a faithful narration of the treatment inflicted on the great man by Sir Hudson Lowe and his subordinates, and that I have even suppressed a few facts which, though true, might have been considered so exaggerated that they would not have been given credence"[53]... Yet, notes O'Méara, the island suffered from a water supply problem: "The water carried to Longwood during the two or three months of summer was extremely cloudy, thick and disgusting; I am convinced that it contributed greatly to the dysentery so common on the island. It is so rare that the soldiers of the 66th Regiment are exhausted to obtain it, being obliged to go and fetch some a league from their camp"[54]. For a long time, Longwood was without any water other than that brought in barrels, dragged on a cart by Chinese, until the end of 1819.

Even today, the *Institut Pasteur* website recommends hepatitis A and B vaccinations for long-stay visitors to St. Helena. There is no vaccine against hepatitis E. However, hepatitis A and E are transmitted oro-fecally by drinking

53. MARCHAND Joseph, *Mémoires*, published by Jean Bourguignon and Henry Lachouque, Tallandier, 1985, T. II, p. 405, among the notes.
54. O'Meara Barry E., *Relation des événements arrivés à Sainte-Hélène postérieurement à la nomination de Sir Hudson Lowe au gouvernement de cette île*, Chaumont jeune, 1819, p. 38.

water contaminated with faeces. If the hepatitis virus is still present on the island today, despite the construction of a water supply system, we can only imagine what the sanitary conditions were like almost two centuries ago!

What's more, Longwood was teeming with rats to an unimaginable degree, as the house was built on the ground, a clayey chalk covered only by a floor. One day, the Emperor picked up his hat and a rat escaped. Rats and their fleas transmit numerous infectious diseases: typhus, leptospirosis, plague, tularemia, Haverhil fever, etc.

O'Méara inspected the parish registers, which "prove the truth of this assertion: they show that very few people live beyond the age of forty-five"[55].

The French were not the only ones concerned: "I affirm on my honor," continues O'Meara, "that 56 men of the second battalion of the sixty-sixth regiment, in the twelve or thirteen months of their stay on St. Helena, died of dysentery or hepatitis"[56].

And further on: "In twelve or thirteen months, one battalion out of 630 men lost 56, which makes one out of twelve; an unheard-of mortality in any of our colonies, where it gives only two out of seventy-three"[57].

55. *Op. cit.* p. 74.
56. *Op. cit.* p. 61.
57. *Op. cit.* p. 74.

Similarly, in July 1817, *Le Conquérant* lost 110 of its full complement of 600 men (plus 107 sailors sent back to England).

Gourgaud, on April 16, 1817, notes "in the last seven days, four soldiers have died of dysentery"[58]. And on April 28, 1817, "There are many sick people in town; in the camp, several soldiers have died"[59].

What's more, as is often the case on the islands, St. Helena's climate varies greatly depending on whether you're upwind (wet) or downwind (drier). Napoleon's residence, Longwood, is exposed to the wind, at 1800-2000 feet above sea level (around 580 m). "The thermometer at Longwood marks 53° Farenheit (that's 12° Celsius) up to 80° (27° Celsius) in the shade, 86° (30° Celsius) at three in the afternoon when the sun is in the northwest (we're in the southern hemisphere)."

The only vegetation is *Conyza Gummifera,* which provides little shade and attracts flies. The humid trade winds blow constantly from the southeast. This alternation of temperature and humidity perpetually gives Napoleon a cold.

O'Meara affirms: "If Lord Bathurst or Sir Hudson Lowe had wished Napoleon to be suitably and as pleasantly housed as one can be in this miserable island, it was

58. GOURGAUD, *Journal intégral,* Perrin, 2019, p. 403.
59. *Ibid,* p. 415.

necessary to lodge him at the Plantation house which is the best, or to build him one at Rosemary Hall, or near Colonel Smith's where there is shade and water, and where one is sheltered from the south-east wind"[60].

Plantation House is a vast house sheltered from the wind, with a portico overlooking a vast meadow surrounded by woods. Installing Napoleon at Plantation House, i.e. at Hudson Lowe's residence, was the best solution. Lord Bathurst was opposed to this solution, but Lowe could overrule him: "I also had a discretionary power which I could use if necessary"[61]. St. Helena is 7,500 km from London as the crow flies, a two- to three-month crossing. Lowe cannot claim not to have thought about it, for Napoleon had Montholon write to him: "If the Emperor had been put in Plantation House, where there are beautiful trees, water, gardens, he would have been as well off as this miserable island can allow"[62].

Just as Octavian relegated Lepidus to the fever-infested coast of Latium, in the hope of quickly freeing up the post of *Pontifex maximus,* did England wish to bring about Napoleon's death? Wasn't the *Directoire* deporting

---

60. O'MEARA Barry E., *Relation des événements arrivés à Sainte-Hélène postérieurement à la nomination de Sir Hudson Lowe au gouvernement de cette île,* Chaumont jeune, 1819, p. 235.
61. LOWE Hudson, *Mémorial de sir Hudson Lowe: relatif à la captivité de Napoléon à Sainte-Hélène,* p. 278.
62. *Ibid,* p. 67.

its opponents en masse to French Guiana, so that the “dry guillotine” of the climate and tropical diseases could rid it of them?

13. From What and by Whose Hand Did Napoleon Die?

There are repetitions of chapter 3 here, but as Rivarol used to say, between the inconvenience of repeating oneself and the inconvenience of not being clear, there's no need to swing.

Antommarchi first examined Napoleon on September 23, 1819.

A Doctor of Philosophy and Medicine from the University of Pisa in 1808, Antommarchi hails from Cape Corsica. Doctor of Surgery in 1812, he was appointed Professor of Anatomy at the Academy of Pisa. Antommarchi had the opportunity to confer with O'Méara in London, documenting and discussing his patient's case with numerous English colleagues. Deemed flippant and presumptuous, his *Memoirs* are incomplete, lacking the first half of 1820. I confess to having a soft spot for Antommarchi, a man who was not afraid to cross oceans to treat Napoleon despite the unanimous disapproval he incurred. Contrary to the condescending comments of non-medical historians, Antommarchi was a fine practitioner, the equivalent of what we call a "prosector of anatomy", a flattering title given to future hospital surgeons.

*

If Antommarchi sometimes draws the line, when he confines himself to medicine, he is irreplaceable. Thus, he notes in this first review:

> *The part of the left lobe of the liver corresponding to the epigastric region was as if hardened, extremely painful to pressure. The gall bladder was full, resistant, protruding outside the right hypochondrium, near the cartilage of the third false rib […]. Napoleon felt extreme discomfort in his right shoulder. His breathing became more difficult when pressure was exerted perpendicular to the scrobicule (dimple) of the heart. He also complained of a pain of variable intensity that had long affected the right hypochondrium […] He had nausea and vomiting. [Urination, though frequent, was natural. Abundant sweating occurred daily.*

Antommarchi also notes a sandy tongue, slow pulse at sixty per minute, yellow conjunctiva, overweight, dry cough.

Dr. John Stokoe, on January 19, 1819, had written in his report: "I am now convinced that this viscera [the liver] is seriously affected". For writing this, he was hauled before Lowe's Board of War and struck off the Navy rolls.

Antommarchi, passing through London before setting sail for St. Helena, had consulted his English colleagues, including the venerable James Curry who, having deliberated on the reports by O'Méara and Stokoe, had concluded: "Napoleon is suffering from chronic hepatitis", recommending the use of mercurials, cholagogic drugs that facilitate the elimination of bile through the bile ducts.

What's more, on October 10, 1819, Antommarchi visited the James Town hospital and noted: "It was nothing but dysentery, acute and chronic hepatitis".

*

On November 16, 1819, Napoleon asked Antommarchi about stomach cancer. He was thinking of his father Charles, who had died in Montpellier of *squirrhosis* of the pylorus (a cancerous tumor that is hard to palpate) at just thirty-eight years of age:

"You don't think this kind of affliction is transmitted with life?"

The next day, Antommarchi found him, a medical book in his hand, "preoccupied, dreamy... Napoleon feared he was suffering from the affliction that had brought his father to the grave".

The following year saw a long succession of improvements and deterioration, punctuated by incidents of varying degrees of severity: erysipelas with joint damage, scurvy with gum complications.

*

By July 1820, the Emperor thought he had recovered, but by September 1820, the notorious pain in the right hypochondrium radiating to the shoulder (*phrenic,* as third-year medical students know) reappeared, and for six months Napoleon's health continued to deteriorate. The Emperor was exhausted by the return of all these symptoms, accompanied by invincible fatigue and drowsiness. His extremities were cold.

On October 22, he thought he was cured for a moment, but by October 25, he was exclaiming: "I'm at the end of my rope, I can feel it, and don't kid yourself."

On October 29, evacuation of fairly well-colored matter. If feces appear like this, it's because they were poorly colored before, an argument for lithiasis and against viral hepatitis.

November 1: Liver pain increased. Further transient improvement.

On November 19, he moans: "The bed has become a place of delight for me, I wouldn't exchange it for all the thrones in the world. What a change ! How I have fallen! I, whose activity was boundless, whose head never slumbered! I'm plunged into a lethargic stupor, I have to make an effort when I want to lift my eyelids. Sometimes I dictated on different subjects to four or five secretaries, who went as fast as I could speak, but then I was Napoleon, now I'm nothing".

On January 22, 1821, "all that is lost now I feel, but not yet without resources". He tries his hand at exercise by riding a horse. "I see it now, [...] my strength is failing me, nature no longer responds as before to the solicitations of my will, violent jolts no longer suit my weakened body ; but I will reach the goal I wish to attain by moderate exercise".

January 29, 1821: Napoleon complained bitterly about his doctor: "... Antommarchi is an ignoramus, not a reliable man. He repeats what he hears : it's violating the first duty of his state, he mounts Mme Bertrand's head. [...], because he has against him, this man, that he is a bad doctor, that he doesn't understand the finer points, that he doesn't understand French"[63].

63. MONTHOLON Charles-Tristan, *Récits de la captivité de l'empereur Napoléon à Sainte-Hélène*, tome 9, 1847, p. 629.

On February 9, Montholon and Bertrand obtained a pardon for Antommarchi, whom Napoleon had wanted to expel.

*

His last carriage ride took place on March 17, 1821 ; on the same day, the fever set in. It was to stay with him for the next forty-eight days.

March 19, after a short lull, fever and chills reappear.

March 20: "We must prepare ourselves for the fatal sentence; you, Hortense and I are destined to suffer it on this ugly rock [...] the three of us will meet again on the Champs-Élysées".

On March 25, the fever subsided, and "the Emperor is already talking of an imminent recovery". Napoleon then tells Grand Marshal Bertrand that Montholon is ill and confesses that he can no longer guard him ; that he would like Vignali to guard him. The Grand Marshal said that the Emperor could do no better ; that Vignali was in good health, a bit of a doctor, and an excellent nurse[64].

April 16: Pulse irregular. He shut himself up for two to four hours with Montholon and Marchand. Apparently

64. General BERTRAND, *Cahiers de Sainte-Hélène,* Albin Michel, 1949, vol. 1, p. 119.

working on his final arrangements. He calls Vignali and spends three quarters of an hour with him[65].

The Emperor sends for Vignali. He enters. He hands him the three wills: "Here is my handwritten will. Put your signature and arms here, as well as on the boxes". Vignali bows deeply and passes into the bedroom[66].

Vignali having finished, the Emperor dismissed the Grand Marshal and Vignali remained with the Emperor. In the evening, Napoleon tells Montholon that Vignali has taken the will. He asked what the Grand Marshal had to say. "Nothing, he didn't utter a word"[67].

April 21, Holy Saturday:

At 1 a.m., "the Emperor," says Montholon, "expressed a desire to talk with Abbé Vignali, and ordered me to send for him, adding:

"You'll leave us, but you'll come back as soon as he's out of my room. Make sure no one knows I saw him last night."

I obeyed. Abbé Vignali stayed with the Emperor for an hour[68] [...]. He was still asleep at six o'clock when Marchand came to relieve me."

---

65. *Op.cit.* p. 122.
66. *Op.cit.* p. 127.
67. *Op.cit.* p. 128.
68. MONTHOLON Charles-Tristan, *Récits de la captivité de l'empereur Napoléon à Sainte-Hélène*, tome 2, p. 528.

Marchand: “He found enough strength to get up and spend three hours, partly dictating and partly writing [...]. At half past one (in the afternoon), he asked for Abbé Vignali.”

“Do you know, Abbé, what burning at the stake is”

“Yes, sire.”

“Have you observed any?”

“None.”

“Well, you’ll be doing mine a disservice.”

That same day, says Marchand, Napoleon said “that he wanted his last days to be like the rest of his life: Abbé Vignali would say mass and recite the prayers of the Quarante-Heures, and when he did so, he would have to be left alone with him”.

April 22: The Emperor has mass celebrated. It’s Easter Day.

Dr Arnott has patients to see and can’t come to Mass.

In his will, Napoleon declared that he would die in the Catholic religion of his birth; he declared that before his death Abbé Vignali would give him communion, extreme unction and all that is customary in such cases; he had asked him if he knew what to do.

April 25: Vomiting of black blood mixed with food.

April 26: Napoleon begins to be delirious. Memory lapses. Previously, Napoleon had never been delirious.

On April 27, Napoleon dictated the letter Montholon was to send Lowe announcing his death.

April 28: Napoleon ordered Antommarchi to carry out an autopsy after his death, to examine the stomach thoroughly and make a precise report to his son. Despite his reluctance, he changes to the salon as his bedroom.

April 29: Montholon tries to get him to sign one last paper. He can no longer see the Grand Marshal in front of him. Bertrand weeps: "Voilà le grand Napoléon, miserable, humble."

April 30: Last night, the Emperor retained his sanity. He woke up shouting: *Ah! ah! death!* He said to Montholon: "My friend, I am dead".

There is no longer any immediate danger ! Antommarchi had thought he was going to pass, from ten to eleven o'clock[69].

May 1: At 2 p.m., the fever subsides.

Bertrand: "The Grand Marshal went out at half past one and came back at half past two. The Emperor asked where he had been. In the meantime, M. Vignali had the altar erected, spent a few moments alone with the Emperor and gave him extreme unction."

Antommarchi talks about May 3, 2 a.m.: "The fever is subsiding. We retire. Vignali remains alone, and joins us a few moments later in the next room, where he announces that he has administered the viaticum to the Emperor.

---

69. *Op.cit.* p. 182.

Marchand: "About half an hour later, the abbot came out and said to me: 'The Emperor has just been administered, the state of his stomach does not allow any other sacrament'".

Montholon: "This morning, as I was leaving the Emperor after writing under his dictation for more than two hours, he told me to send Vignali to him; an hour later, the chapel was set up and the chaplain had begun the prayers of the Forty Hours[70].

"In the meantime, Mr. Vignali had the altar erected, spent a few moments alone with the Emperor and gave him extreme unction."

On the subject of communion, Ali and Marchand concur in their account of the invention of Abbé Vignali, who was summoned to the Emperor's bedside, but Marchand points out that the Abbé, in bourgeois attire, was holding something under his clothing that he sought to conceal and that I did not try to guess, thinking well that he had just performed a religious act".

However, Napoleon wished to receive communion[71].

---

70. MONTHOLON Charles-Tristan, *Histoire de la captivité de Sainte-Hélène,* Brockhaus & Avenarius, 1846.

71. "Dernière conversation de Sainte-Hélène: l'Empereur commente son testament", *Revue des Deux Mondes,* XCVIIe année, septième période, tome 48, 1928, pp. 849-875 /Grand Maréchal Bertrand, Ernest d'Hauterive.

May 2: Napoleon repeated his recommendation to examine his stomach and compare it with the autopsy report on his father. The doctor and the two generals are exhausted.

Bertrand: "In the middle of the night, Napoleon wants to get up. Montholon and Vignali took him by the arm. Then Vignali left him, knelt down and prayed"[72]. The Emperor sighed loudly, with effort, and then said: "My God! My God!" Pulse up to 108 (the patient has probably gone into atrial fibrillation).

Montholon dismisses Vignali, while the doctors, the Maréchal and Marchand are in the bedroom. This leaves the wake to be settled[73].

May 3: Short-lived improvement.

May 5: Vignali is present with the others. The children burst into his room. At 5:49 a.m., Napoleon dies. At 10 a.m., Abbé Vignali says a few prayers.

*

Napoleon and the French who accompanied him were not exaggerating when they claimed that the Emperor had been exiled to an unhealthy island. Yet the English had

---

72. *Op.cit.* p. 187.
73. General BERTRAND, *Cahiers de Sainte-Hélène*, Albin Michel, tome 1, 1949, p. 188.

a vested interest in keeping the Napoleon card in their pockets, to influence the Bourbons, and Hudson Lowe, a personal interest in keeping his position as long as possible. But Lowe was a minor civil servant, a staff scribe of limited ideas, terrorized by Lord Bathurst, aggravating his instructions with his intemperate zeal and lack of initiative.

*

The autopsy of 1821, which concluded that Napoleon had suffered from stomach disease, was drawn up following a compromise with the English doctors, in order to minimize the existence of hepatitis and delay publication of the truth as long as possible. Antommarchi refused to countersign it and, in his book of *Memoirs*, he re-established the truth[74]:

> *The spleen and hardened liver were very enlarged and engorged with blood; the liver tissue, reddish-brown in color, showed no notable structural alterations. Extremely thick, lumpy bile filled and distended the gallbladder. The liver, affected by* chronic hepatitis *was tightly bound on its convex surface to the diaphragm; the adhesion extended throughout its entire extent, and was strong, dense and old.*

74. Antommarchi François (Dr), *Mémoires*, Barrois l'aîné, 1825.

And these findings were was so well established that Lowe or his "dyers"[75] wrote in his *Memorial* (admittedly partly questionable from the point of view of authenticity): "Napoleon was attacked by hepatitis or chronic liver disease, then reached at its highest level of intensity. This disease, according to Beatson and M. Jennings, who have particularly studied the climatic temperature of St. Helena, is endemic at this latitude, and very often fatal"[76].

*

It's true that the stomach lesions were confirmed by the autopsy, but in the absence of an anatomopathological examination, which didn't exist at the time, it's impossible to formally confirm the diagnosis of stomach cancer, especially as Napoleon was still overweight. What's more, the five-year duration of the disease from 1816 to 1821 is more consistent with chronic hepatitis than with stomach cancer, which lasts a relatively short twelve months.

The most salient aspect of O'Meara and Antommarchi's medical observation is this:

75. Teinturier: nègre, in literature, as Alexandre Dumas put it, or porte-plume, as the politically correct would have it.
76. LOWE Hudson, *Mémorial relatif à la captivité de Napoléon à Sainte-Hélène*, L.Dureuil, 1830, p. 357.

1. Napoleon died after a long fever, with shivering and sweating, which lasted for forty-eight days ;

2. he died with a low small bowel obstruction.

Let's start again.

1. If this long-term fever is due to an infectious cause: there are only three possible infections: endocarditis, tuberculosis or brucellosis.

Brucellosis may explain hepatosplenomegaly, but is unlikely, as contamination almost always occurs through consumption of milk from infected cattle. It is well known that Napoleon hated drinking milk.

Infective endocarditis is the best explanation for the infectious syndrome and jaundice with hepatosplenomegaly, pleural effusion and edema of the lower limbs. The germ's obvious point of entry is the teeth, which are in a deplorable state following scurvy, or the urinary tract. However, Antommarchi makes it clear: "The orifices of the heart do not present any notable lesions". Admittedly, Osler had not yet described the acute infective endocarditis that now bears his name, and Laennec had not yet laid the foundations of cardiac auscultation, but it seems impossible that an anatomist of Antommarchi's quality would not have seen possible vegetations on the heart valves.

That leaves *tuberculosis,* a hypothesis made all the more plausible by the doctor's observation of "an upper (left) lobe dotted with tubercles and a few small tubercular excavations", with a bilateral pleural effusion of a citrine (i.e. inflammatory) color. Tuberculosis may explain the enlarged liver and spleen, as well as the low occlusion by functional ileus, as there was a "soft, transparent, diffluent exudation, coating in their entire extent the two ordinarily contiguous parts of the inner face of the peritoneum". However, the tongue had a thick, white coating ; tuberculosis, it remains clean.

Antommarchi noted, in addition to the perforated ulcer blocked by the left lobe of the liver—and thus healed—a cancerous ulcer at the top of the lesser curvature, but also that chronic hepatitis that everyone expected to find. And even in the absence of anatomopathological microscopic examination, which today is the only way to make a decision, it corresponds so well to the clinical description, with its pain in the right hypochondrium radiating towards the right shoulder, that there is really no reason to hesitate. Napoleon was suffering from chronic viral hepatitis and a stomach ailment, either cancerous or tubercular.

2. Second salient point: Napoleon died of small intestinal obstruction with severe abdominal distention. However, the stomach lesions did not lead to total food intolerance. The autopsy states that "the orifice of the pylorus was in a perfectly normal state" and that the "annular squirrhous hardening" did not impede the passage of food. I don't

know why my colleague Jacques di Constanzo refers to a perforation of the stomach, as there would indeed have been "communication between the stomach cavity and that of the abdomen had the adhesion with the liver not been in the way". However, "the adhesion of this part [of the stomach] to the left lobe of the liver blocked the opening". What's more, if the stomach ulcer had perforated, there would have been a clear abdominal contracture. Lastly, a low occlusion can only be explained by an obstacle located from or beyond the second jejunum, and gastric lesions cannot account for it. This occlusion is therefore secondary to diffuse peritoneal inflammation, and as Antommarchi did not find an abscess, we must invoke an inflammation of intraperitoneal organs: the liver, the stomach or both, or an intestinal perforation. Note the involvement of the lesser omentum: "the lymph glands [...] placed along the curves of the stomach [...] were partly swollen, indurated, some even suppurating".

There are three related hypotheses:

1. leptospirosis transmitted by rats. It causes liver damage, fever and splenomegaly, but the duration of the disease is shorter ;

2. acute angiocholitis, i.e. an infection originating in the bile ducts. Dr. Jacques di Constanzo insisted on this hypothesis, which fits in well with the clinical picture, but

the autopsy report, while noting a dilated vesicle filled with thick bile, does not note any vesicular calculi. Constanzo tells us that this is possible, and we readily believe him, but we would be more comfortable affirming it in the opposite case[77];

3. an upper urinary tract infection, as there is bladder lithiasis and the urine is muddy. But in this case, the pain of pyelonephritis is frankly posterior in the costo-lumbar angle. Moreover, the kidneys were normal at autopsy.

*

The reader will recall that I had received three samples of Napoleon tendon from Mr. Sou Mong. Fragment C was used. How was this small, apparently richly vascularized sample going to help me uncover the truth?

A few years ago, I developed a PCR test for Claude Lévy Laboratories in Paris, enabling the identification of hepatitis B virus DNA[78]. Microscopy of the sample showed the

---

77. Di Costanzo Jacques, "À propos des maladies de Napoléon à Sainte-Hélène: les pathologies digestives", *Revue du Souvenir napoléonien*, no433, February-March 2001, pp. 34-37.
78. Lucotte Gérard, Galzot Pierre, Y Lu Chen, Bathelier Christian, Champenois, Thierry, "Detection of serum hepatitis B virus assay a nested polymerase chain reaction assay", *Molecular and Cellular Probes*, December 8 (6), 1994, pp. 437-440.

presence of vessels, and therefore of blood (figure 20). I entrusted the sample to the laboratory technician:

"Here's a sample that weighs next to nothing," I told him, "but whose significance is heavy for history."

I have a right to say historic things, too.

The PCR technique was used once again, with the usual precautions. The result: Napoleon was positive for the hepatitis B virus.

*

I don't believe in the cancer hypothesis because of the Emperor's overweight. I admit the possibility of acute angiocholitis. Perhaps an intestinal perforation, although Antommarchi doesn't mention this. And pulmonary tuberculosis had probably also been reactivated. But it is no less true that Napoleon was suffering from chronic viral hepatitis, in line with the convergent opinion of the clinicians who approached him, Barry O'Meara, John Stokoe, Francesco Antommarchi: typical pain described many times, appearance at autopsy, revealed once the governor's attempts at intimidation had disappeared, presence of hepatitis B virus.

Right up to the end, the English, in the person of Hudson Lowe, sought—even to the point of depriving him of a doctor and medical care for months on end—both to conceal the reality of the liver damage and to minimize the endemic presence of dysentery and chronic hepatitis on the island of St. Helena.

And all this while housing their prisoner in the most insalubrious part of the island, exposed to the trade winds and devoid of drinking water.

Finally, if the anecdote recounted by Prof. René Leriche is accurate[79] (and we have no reason to doubt it, even though the evidence disappeared during the *Blitz*), their direct responsibility is engaged.

*

The young Bonaparte wrote it wistfully on the wall of his room at the *École Militaire*: "Everything always ends up six feet under".

Antivirals date back mainly to the 1980s. The first anti-tuberculosis drugs appeared after the Second World War. Stomach cancer was not curable at the time (it is hardly curable today).

Hepatitis, stomach cancer or tuberculosis, Napoleon was doomed in the short term. But was this a reason to prevent him from treating himself? To leave him without a doctor for nine months in 1819?

---

79. Vox Maximilien, *Napoléon*, Le temps qui court, 1959.

*

“I die prematurely, murdered by the English oligarchy and its paymaster,” wrote the Emperor in his will.

That’s exactly the truth.

14. Appendices and Documents

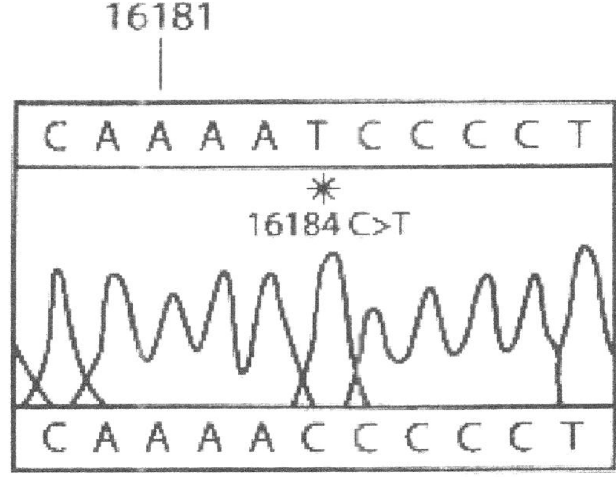

Figure 1: The 16184C->T mutation, as discovered by DNA sequencing of a portion of the hypervariable 1 sequence of Napoleon's mtDNA. In this portion, the DNA base alignment is marked by position 16181, with the bottom alignment representing the normal base sequence and the top representing the mutation sequence. The peaks of the C to T sequence are visible, as is that of the T base in the mutant sequence.

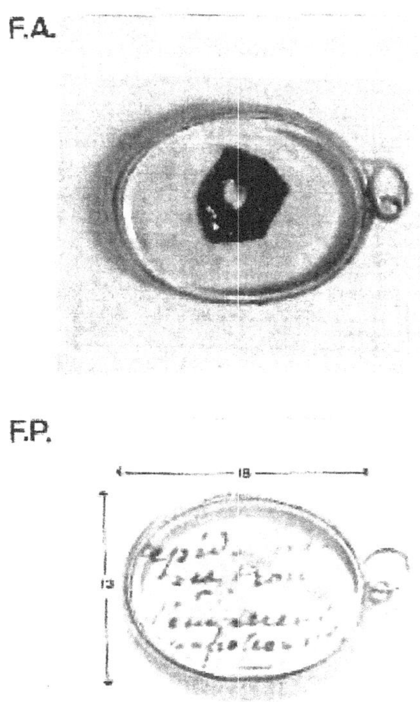

Figure 2: Photographs of the anterior (F.A.) and posterior (F.P.) faces of Dr. Guillard's medallion. The writing is visible on the posterior surface (dimensions: 18 and 13 mm). The whitish epidermis is visible on the anterior surface ; it has been deposited on a small black piece to enhance contrast.

Figure 3: Scanning electron microscope photographs of a portion of Napoleon's hair (magnified × 30,000) *above*, and of his mother (magnified × 1,000) *on the following page* ; the scales, arranged in transverse rows, are clearly visible. Below each photograph are the EDX spectra resulting from X-ray microfluorescence analysis, taken from the middle part of the hair (circle). Each spectrum is represented as a distribution of values, where peaks correspond to the signal intensity and characterization (in kilobases) on the horizontal axis of each element.

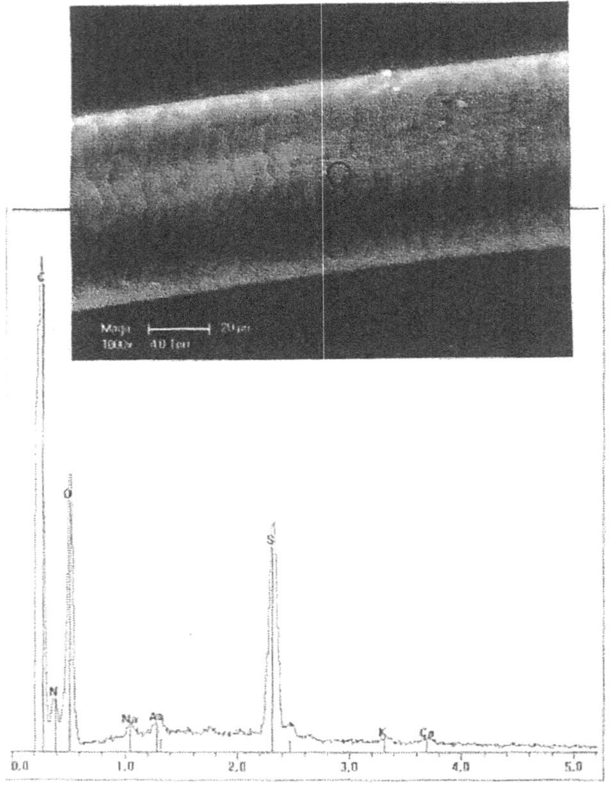

Figure 3 (continued): Both spectra show peaks of carbon (C), nitrogen (N) and oxygen (O), corresponding to the organic matter in the hair; sulfur (S), corresponding to the disulfide bridges in the hair's keratin; and small peaks corresponding to traces of sodium (Na), chlorine (Cl), potassium (K) and calcium (Ca). Only the spectrum of Napoleon's mother's hair contains arsenic (As).

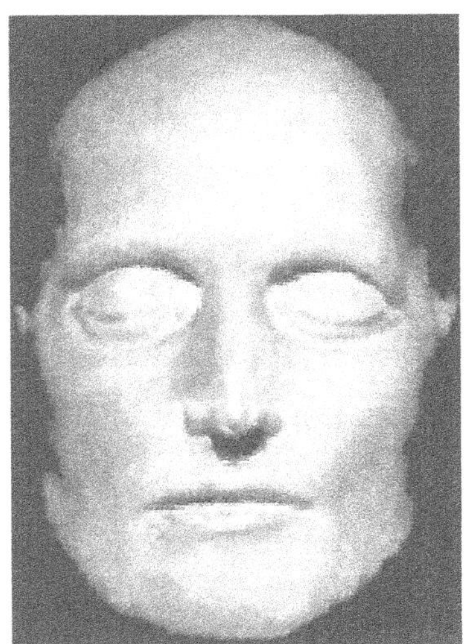

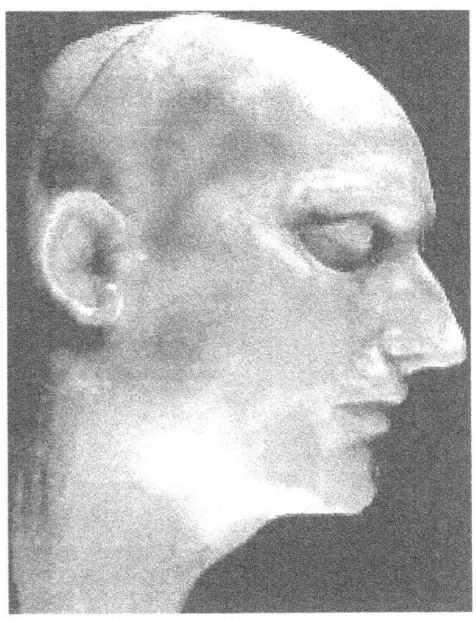

Figure 4: Photographs (front and right profile) of the Noverraz 2 mask.

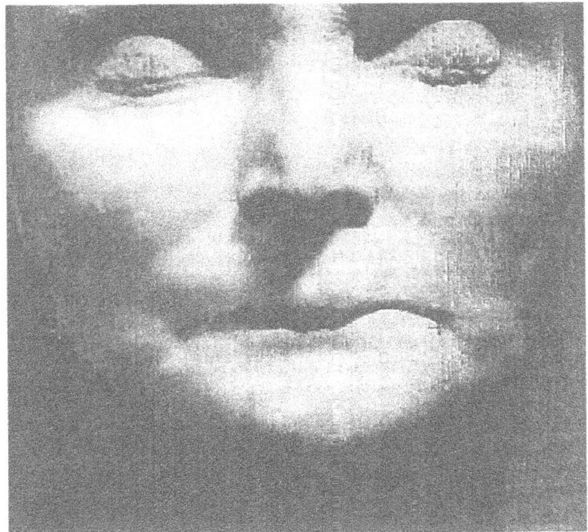

Figure 5: Front view of the RUSI mask.

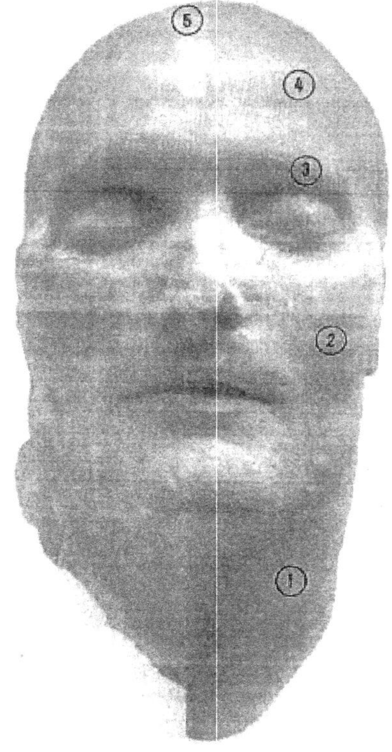

Figure 6: Photograph of the Azémar mask. The circles numbered 1 to 4 correspond to the areas of the mask where plaster samples were taken.

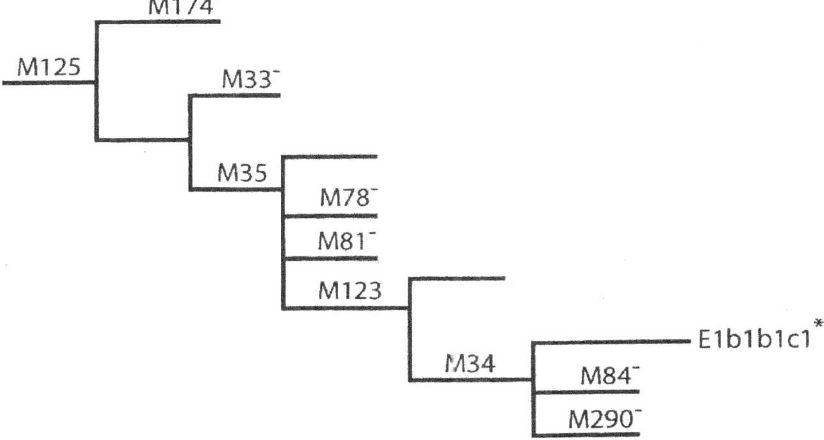

Figure 7: This figure shows the hierarchy of the successive use of these markers already described in the scientific literature; the resulting haplotype is indeed E1b1b1c1, the terminal SNP marker of differentiation being M13.

Successive order of markers used to determine the Napoleon haplotype. The first marker present is M125 (it is verified that M174 is negative) ; the second is M35 (it is verified that M33 is negative); then it is shown that M123 is present (M81 and M78 are negative). The terminal marker of differentiation is M34 (M84 and M290 are negative) ; the resulting haplotype is: E1b1b1c1.

Locus	Y-STRs	Napoléon I	Charles Napoléon
1	DYS393		14
2	DYS390		24
3	DYS19*	13	13
4	DYS391		10
5	DYS385a		16
6	DYS385b		16
7	DYS426		11
8	DYS388		12
9	DYS439		12
10	DYS389-1		14
11	DYS392		11
12	DYS389-2		31
13	DYS458		19
14	DYS459a		9
15	DYS 459b		9
16	DYS455		11
17	DYS454		7
18	DYS447		21
19	DYS437		14
20	DYS448		20
21	DYS449		28
22	DYS464a**		14
23	DYS464b**		15
24	DYS464c**		16
25	DYS464d**		17
26	DYS460		10
27	DYSGATAH4		11
28	DYSYCAIIa	19	19

29	DYSYCAIIb	22	22
30	DYS456		15
31	DYS607		12
32	DYS576		18
33	DYS570		19
34	DYSCDYa		35
35	DYSCDYb		36
36	DYS442		12
37	DYS438		10

Figure 8: The table above shows the Y-STR profile of Charles Napoleon based on 37 Y-STR markers (locus 1 to 37) ; the allelic values for each marker are given by numbers. Napoleon's allelic values are the same for three of these markers (one star indicates a discriminating value for haplotype E1b1b, and two stars a highly discriminating value for this haplotype.

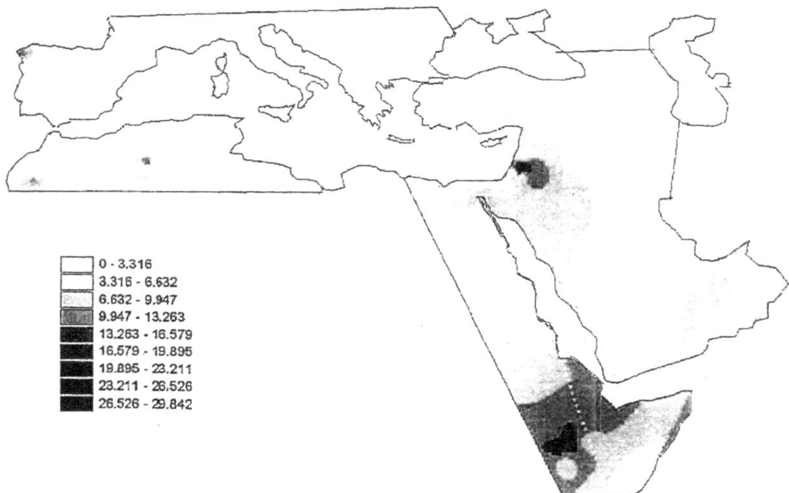

Figure 9: Numerically processed values for the percentages of men carrying the M13 marker in populations from the Middle East, North Africa and north-west Spain. The two grey scales indicate the increasing percentages encountered.

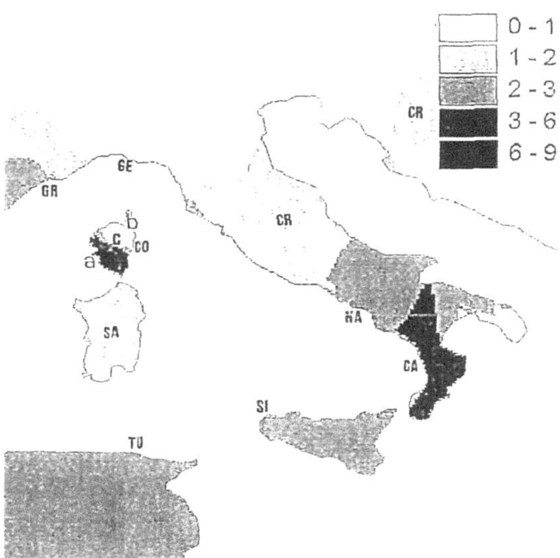

Figure 10: Numerical values for percentages of men carrying the M13 marker in populations from mainland Italy, Sicily, Tunisia, Sardinia, Corsica and part of south-eastern France. Five gradations of gray are shown.

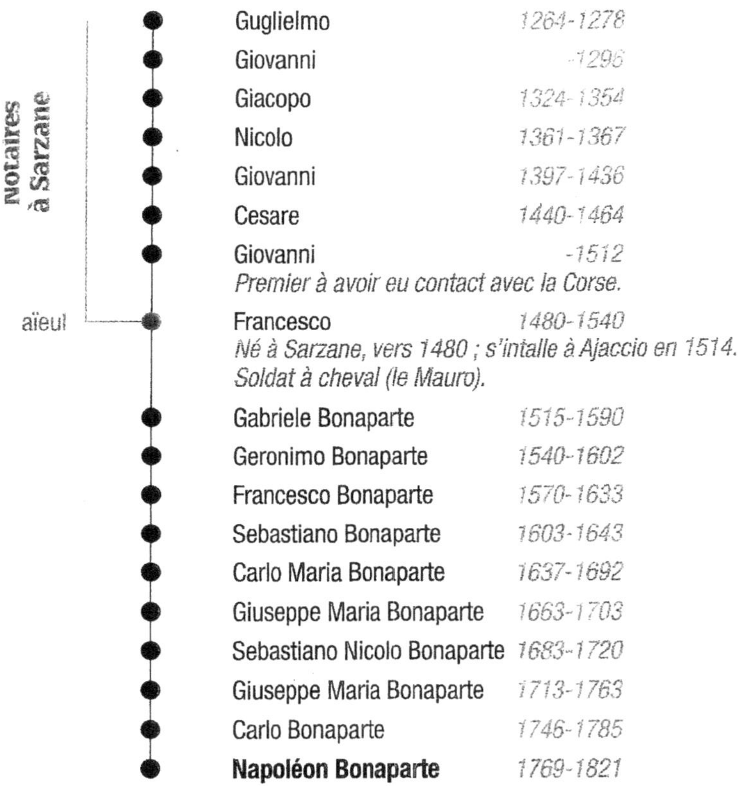

Figure 11: 17-generation paternal ancestry of Napoleon Bonaparte. Dates of birth and death are shown where known.

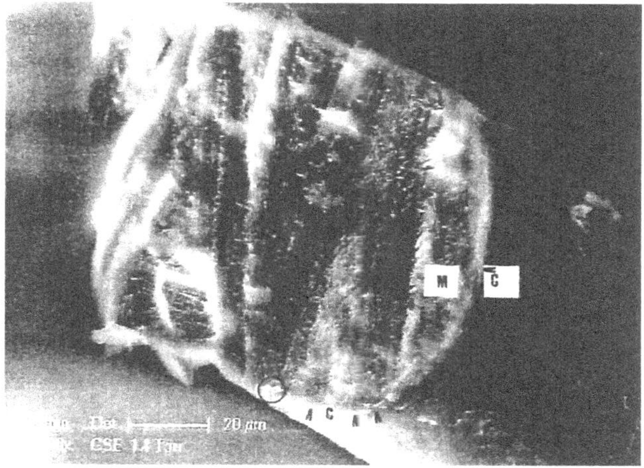

Figure 12: I checked this freckle with an electron microscope ; melanosomes, corpuscles containing grains of melanin, are present in her hair in two forms:

- type 1, shaped like a grain of rice, contains black eumelanin;
- pheomelanin type 2, between yellow and brown.

But these are more numerous in the superficial layers of the hair, which ultimately results in a reddish color. Note once again the fineness of this hair, with an average thickness of only 50 to 60µ.

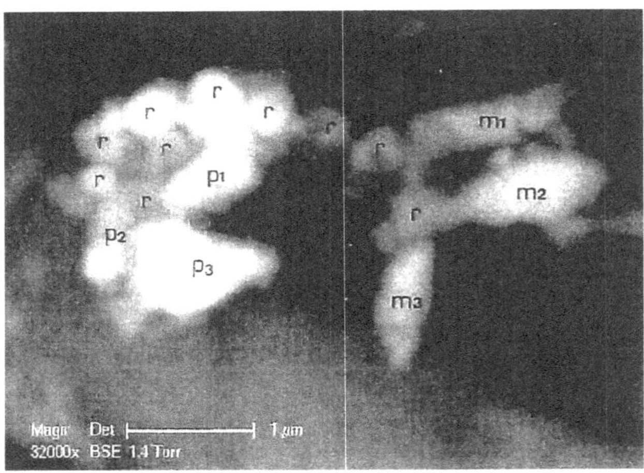

Figure 12 (continued):

Scanning electron microscopy photographs of melanosomes on the surface of a slice of Napoleon's hair:

- *previous page* (× 1,000): the hair slice (C cortex; M matrix); the arrows indicate the regions of the cortex that have been cut; the small circle is enlarged in the bottom photograph.
- *above* (× 32,000): the enlarged region of the circle showing melanosomes. Corpuscles m1, m2, m3 are eumelanosomes; p1, p2, p3 are pheomelanosomes.

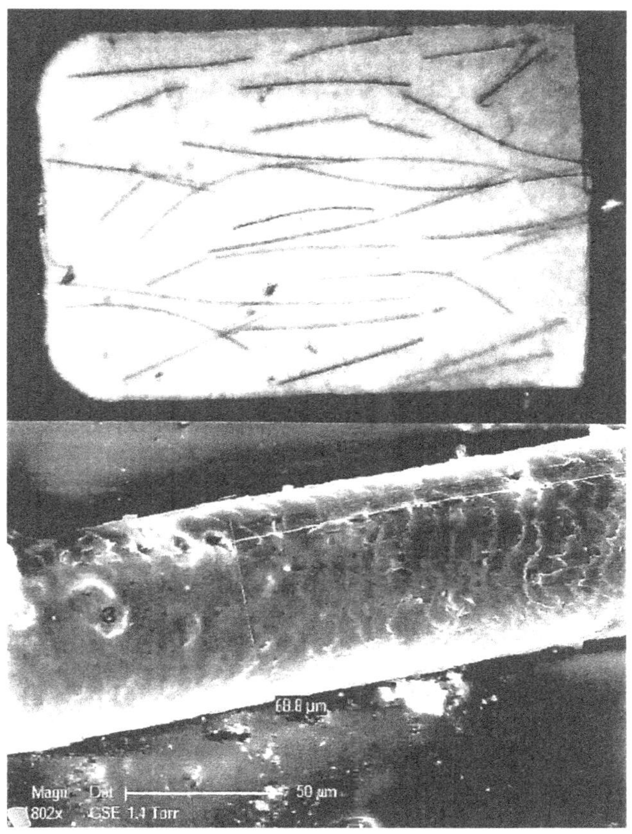

Figure 13: These photographs illustrate the two characteristics of Napoleon's hair. *Top* (light microscopy × 20): freckling, on a few dozen hair fragments (visible only on the original photographs). *Bottom* (scanning electron microscopy × 802): fineness. The hair shown measures 68.8 μ in diameter.

Figure 14: 1803 painting of Bonaparte by François Gérard. Bottom left: 1. pale face, 2. light-blue eyes, 3. hair with reddish highlights (only visible in original shots).

- White skin determined by FF homozygosity of the MATP gene.
- Clear eyes determined by CC homozygosity of a HERC2 gene variant.
- Freckling determined by sequencing the MC1-R gene, where the D294H mutation, the main mutation causing freckling in certain populations, was found in heterozygous state.

Figure 15: Flow chart summarizing the similarities and differences between Messrs Clovis and C.Cipollini.

Figure 16: Photograph of the "penis". *Top,* box (B) decorated with a golden N surmounted by a crown. *Below,* the two compartments inside the box: the one on the right contains the anatomical part (P), the one on the left, two envelopes containing the hair.

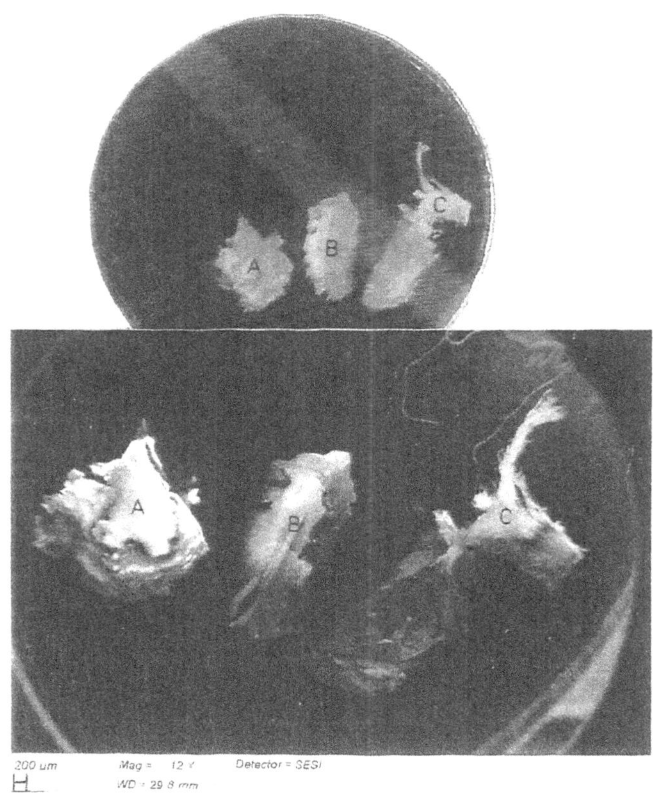

Figure 17: Photographs of the three fragments A, B and C. *Top,* light microscopy. *Bottom,* electron microscopy at low magnification (×12).

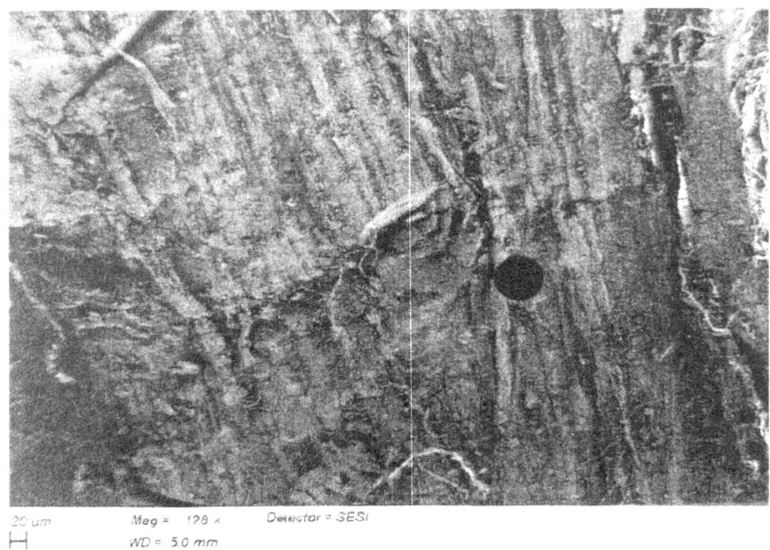

Figure 18: Scanning electron microscope photograph (× 128) of a portion of part 2 of fragment C, showing the longitudinal striations (the black dot indicates the sample surface where EDX analysis was carried out).

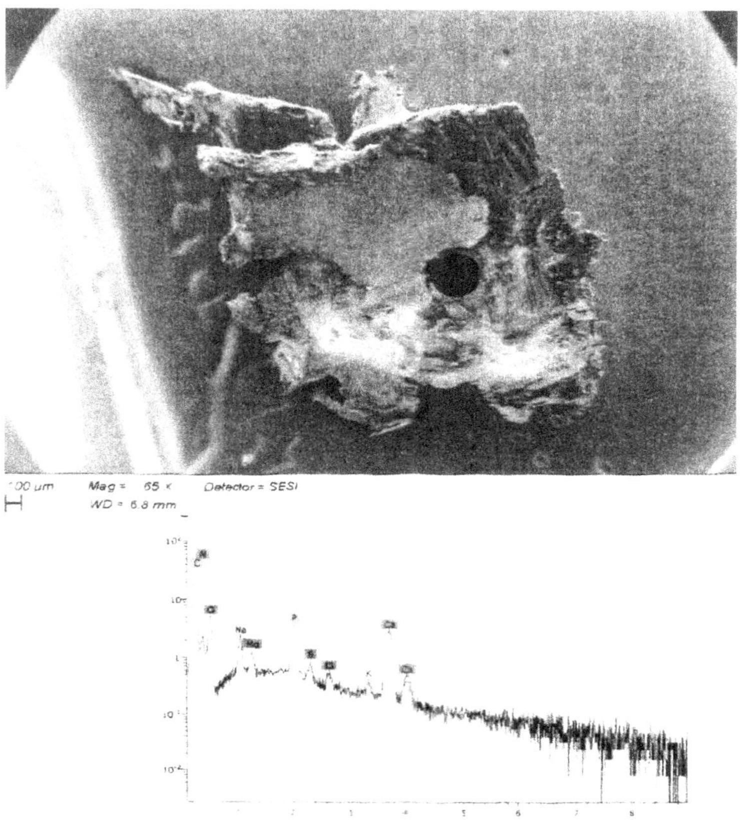

Figure 19: Photograph and EDX analysis of fragment A. *Top:* Scanning electron microscope photograph (× 65) of fragment A: the black dot indicates the surface of this sample where EDX analysis was carried out. *Bottom,* EDX spectrum (in semi-logarithmic coordinates, to better distinguish small element peaks). The elemental peaks are as follows: C: Carbon; N: Nitrogen; O: Oxygen, Na: Sodium; Mg: Magnesium; P: Phosphorus, S: Sulfur: Cl: Chlorine; K: Potassium; Ca (two peaks): Calcium.

Figure 20: Photograph and EDX analysis of fragment C. *Top,* scanning electron microscope photograph (× 72) of a portion of part 1 of fragment C, showing three blood vessels oriented along the longitudinal axis of the piece; the black dot indicates the surface of this sample where EDX analysis was carried out. *Below,* the EDX spectrum, showing elemental peaks. These include phosphorus (P) and calcium (Ca), corresponding to the calcium phosphate in the sample ; the small iron (Fe) peak probably corresponds to the hemoglobin in the red blood cells.

15. Annotated Scientific Bibliography

To help the scientifically-minded reader find his way around, I list here the bibliographical references for the various DNA markers used in the different studies described in this book, and their uses.

A. Mitochondrial DNA (mtDNA)

The 16184T mtDNA mutation characteristic of Napoleon, his mother and his sister Caroline has been published under the reference:

LUCOTTE Gérard, "A rare variant of the mtDNA HSV1 sequence in the hairs of Napoleon family", *Investigative Genetics,* vol. 1, 2010, p. 1-5.

Because of the abundance of mtDNA in cells, this mutation is the most easily detected. It has been used to authenticate Napoleon's remains in a number of cases.

Firstly (unpublished study), in the case of a lock of hair acquired by a private collector, accompanied by an attestation from Antommarchi.

This mutation was also found in an eyebrow hair from the Azéma-Antommarchi death mask:

LUCOTTE Gérard, THOMASSET Thierry, POUGETOUX Alain, "The Napoleon mutation 16184T is that found in the HSV1 sequence of the mtDNA extracted from an eyebrow included in the plaster of the Antommarchi death mask of Napoleon", *International Journal of Sciences*, vol. 4, January 2018, pp. 104-133.

For beard hair on the Noverraz mask (unpublished study) and down between the eyebrows on the RUSI mask, please refer to:

LUCOTTE Gérard, JULLIEN, Frans, THOMASSET Thierry, "The RUSI mask is an authentic replicate of the original death mask of Napoleon", *International Journal of Sciences*, vol. 12(7), January 2023, pp. 55-68.

This mutation has also been found:

- in the hair of a Napoleon hat (unpublished study), which allowed its authentication;

- in the "epidermis" of Napoleon's sample, taken by Dr Guillard when the remains were returned:

LUCOTTE Gérard, THOMASSET Thierry, BORENSZTAJN Stephen, "The medallion of Dr Rémy Guillard (1799-1869) Contains Well Epidermis of Napoleon the First",

International Journal of Sciences, vol.10(11), november 2021, p. 1-6.

- as well as in Napoleon's "penis":

LUCOTTE Gérard, BORENSZTAJN, Stephan, "SEM-EDX and mtDNA analyses of the penis of Napoleon", *International Journal of Sciences*, vol. 11(5), May 2022, pp. 15-21.

B. Y chromosome haplotypes and haplogroups

The first Napoleon SNPs and Charles Napoleon Y-STRs were published:

LUCOTTE Gérard, THOMASSET Thierry, HRECHDAKIAN Peter, "Haplogroupe of Y chromosome of Napoleon the First", *Journal of Molecular Biology Research*, vol. 1, no. 1, December 2011, pp. 12-19.

Alexandre Walewski's complete Y-STRs profile was subsequently published in:

LUCOTTE Gérard, MACÉ Jacques, HRECHDAKIAN Peter, "Reconstruction of the Lineage Y Chromosome Haplotype of Napoleon the First", *International Journal of Sciences*, September 2013, vol. 2(9), p. 127-139.

Finally, a comparison of the S-STR profiles of Charles Napoléon, Alexandre Walewski and Mike Clovis, as well as a reconstruction of Napoléon's, can be found here:

LUCOTTE Gérard, HRECHDAKIAN Peter, "New Advances Reconstructing the Y Chromosome Haplotype of Napoleon the First based on three of his living descendants", *Journal of Molecular Biology Research*, vol. 5(1), 2015, pp. 1-10.

A study on the geographic distribution of the SNP named M34, the terminal SNP marker of Napoleon Y haplotype differentiation has been published here:

LUCOTTE Gérard, DIÉTERLEN Florent, "Frequencies of M34, the Ultimate Genetic Marker of the terminal differenciation of Napoleon the First's Y-Chromosome Haplogroup E1b1b1c1, in Europe, Nothern Africa and the Near East", *International Journal of Anthropology*, 2014, vol. 29, no 1,2,p. 27-41.

The most accomplished study of Napoleon's Y-chromosome AND markers (actually deduced from Mike Clovis) was finally published under the title:

LUCOTTE Gérard, HRECHDAKIAN Peter, SAVARD, Denis, "Towards a full-length Y-chromosome DNA sequence of Napoleon the First: beyond the E-M34 SNP sub-haplogroup", *Austin Journal of Genetics and Genomic Research*, vol. 2(2), 2015, p. 1-4.

This was the basis for M. Grassi's subsequent characterization of one of the three Italian subjects from the Sarzane region (whose family is related to Napoleon's).

C. Autosomal markers

Autosomal markers are those whose DNA is not located on the sex chromosomes (Y and X). We have published on such markers:

LUCOTTE Gérard, BOUIN WILKINSON Alexandra, "An autosomal STR profile of Napoleon the First", *Open Journal of Genetics,* vol. 4, 2014, p. 292-299.

The 14 genetic markers thus described, whose genes are located on various chromosomes, constitute an STR profile that could be used in the future to search for Napoleon's relatives and putative descendants.

Other autosomal gene variants were used in the Napoleon face study:

LUCOTTE Gérard, MACÉ Jacques, THOMASSET Thierry, "Napoleon the First, a Corsican with pale skin, clear eyes and red hair: DNA evidence for these phenotypic traits", *International Journal of Sciences,* vol. 10(7), July 2021, pp. 1-5.

These are the F variant of the MATP gene, the C variant of the HERC2 gene and the D 294H mutation of the MC1-R gene (whose entire sequence has been determined).

Table of Contents

www.ingramcontent.com/pod-product-compliance
Lightning Source LLC
LaVergne TN
LVHW012054160826
845678LV00014B/2821